9/18

D1600986

To Alison, Leiden and Spencer
— *the pearls of my life.*

And In Fond Memory of John Bil

*He stands there, opening the shells with a skill
undreamed of by an ordinary man*

— M.F.K. FISHER, *"Consider the Oyster"*

The Oyster Companion

A SHUCKER'S FIELD GUIDE
FOR CONNOISSEURS

PATRICK McMURRAY

Foreword by Ben Wright and Robin Hancock
The Wright Brothers, Borough, London

Introduction by Sandy Ingber
The Grand Central Oyster Bar & Restaurant

FIREFLY BOOKS

A FIREFLY BOOKS / BLACK WALNUT BOOK

A FIREFLY BOOK

Published by Firefly Books Ltd. 2018

Text © 2018 Patrick McMurray
Design, Compilation and Production
© 2018 Black Walnut Media Limited

All rights reserved. No part of this publication may be reproduced, stored
in a retrieval system, or transmitted in any form or by any means, electronic,
mechanical, photocopying, recording or otherwise, without the prior written
permission of the Publisher.

First printing

Library of Congress Control Number: 2018939512

Library and Archives Canada Cataloguing in Publication
McMurray, Patrick
[Consider the oyster]
    The oyster companion / Patrick McMurray.
Originally published under title: Consider the oyster: a shucker's field guide.
Toronto: McLelland & Stewart, ©2007.
Updated and expanded.
Includes bibliographical references and index.
ISBN 978-0-228-10158-1 (softcover)
    1. Oysters. 2. Oyster culture. 3. Cooking (Oysters). 4. Oysters--
Shucking. I. Title. II. Title: Consider the oyster.
QL430.7.O9M36 2018   639'.41   C2018-901918-2

Published in the United States by
Firefly Books (U.S.) Inc.
P.O. Box 1338, Ellicott Station
Buffalo, New York 14205

Published in Canada by
Firefly Books Ltd.
50 Staples Avenue, Unit 1
Richmond Hill, Ontario L4B 0A7

Front Cover Photography: Tauqir Shah / Big Shah Films
Author photo: Brilynn Ferguson
Back cover photo: Patrick McMurray

This title was produced by
Black Walnut Media Limited
Toronto, Canada
info@blackwalnutlimited.com

Printed in China

 We acknowledge the financial support
of the Government of Canada

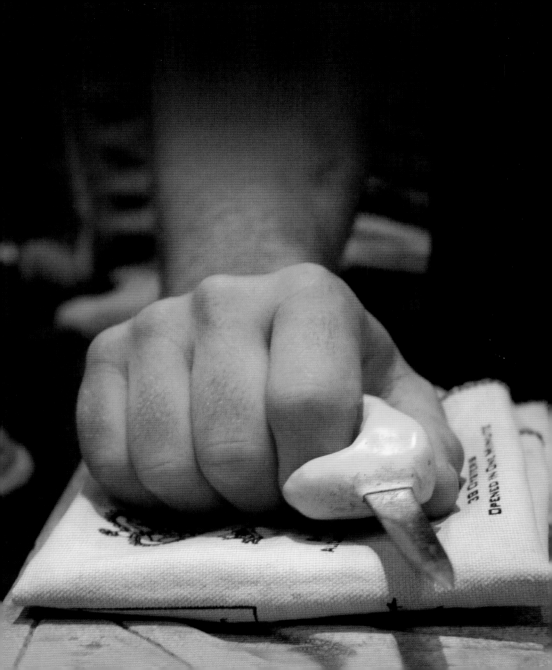

ShuckerPaddy knife in hand, at the ready

Oysters are the eternal and ever-returning call of the sea, of life itself.

BEN WRIGHT & ROBIN HANCOCK
The Wright Bros. Ltd.

Patrick McMurray is more than just a world champion oyster shucker. He is a first-rate advocate for oysters, and an all-round good lad besides. Patrick knows his oysters. And he is passionate about them. We know so well ourselves why this should be so. In 2002, we had other careers when we met Jerome Miet, one of France's great oyster farmers. We decided that becoming purveyors of finest oysters was what we wanted to do. We believed great oysters should be available to everyone. That is still our big idea. We know that is Patrick's passion, too.

We started by telling anyone who would listen about oysters — how they were grown, how they were purified, how good they are for you, and how to shuck, prepare, and, even, how to eat them (chew them and you'll never go back to shooting them straight down). We approached the best chefs — the guys and girls who love working with seafood. They loved how fresh and delicious our oysters were. So did their customers. The word spread and more chefs started to use us as their oyster supplier. We were on to something.

Over on the other side of the Atlantic and around the same time, Patrick McMurray was on to something, too. We first met Shucker Paddy when he was running his now-storied Starfish Oyster Bed and Grill in Toronto. We immediately recognized a fellow connoisseur. He had the same boundless enthusiasm, the same love of oyster lore that we recognize in the best lay scholars of this bounty of our tidal estuaries and shores. We carried copies of his first book in our establishment in the Borough Market, London.

To understand why oysters have such a magical effect on all those who discover their delights and for whom they have become a lifelong passion, it is well to remember where they come from: the sea — the same source of our own origins — and the shores, where our long-ago ancestors once gathered and foraged. As Patrick knows, the delights of oysters are for a lifetime. This may be why legendary oyster aficionado and culinary writer, Keith Floyd, ailing in health but still glorious in spirit, declared after a lunch of champagne and oysters, his final meal: "I've not felt this well in ages."

Ben Wright and Robin Hancock, Wright Bros. Ltd. Borough, London

O Oysters, come and walk with us!
– Lewis Carroll, *The Walrus and the Carpenter*

SANDY INGBER
Executive Chef, Grand Central Oyster Bar & Restaurant

No book about oysters and oyster bars would be complete without some mention of the Oyster Bar in Grand Central Terminal. At least that's how Patrick McMurray put it to us when he first approached us about *The Oyster Companion*. And there's certainly some truth, and a lot of history, in what he says. It was *the* Oyster Bar. Oysters were a cornerstone in the diet of New Yorkers, before they were New Yorkers. Before Europeans ever set eyes on the region, huge piles of oyster shells (called *middens*), some more than fifty feet high, dotted the regional landscape — remnants of the Indigenous people's feasts. The Dutch boasted of the best oysters in the world to their masters back in Amsterdam. The English went further, sending the highly sought-after bivalve back to London by ship. Oysters a foot long were the norm in Gowanus Bay, near present-day Brooklyn.

New York was truly Oyster Nirvana. Reach into the water (with a long-enough pole) and ye shall be fed! As New York grew, so did the city's love affair with the oyster. Oyster cellars sprouted up everywhere. They were often located in the basements of residential buildings, and even the seediest versions saw clientele from every stratum of society.

From the moment the Grand Central Oyster Bar & Restaurant opened its doors in 1913, it attracted incoming and outgoing travelers using the intercontinental railway system, as well as New York City's rich and famous. The restaurant prospered in the Roaring Twenties, persevered through the Great Depression, created countless memories for GIs passing through during the Second World War, and met the challenge of air travel head-on in the 50s. By the 60s, however, the grande dame of the oyster had fallen on hard times. In 1973, restaurant entrepreneur Jerry Brody was beckoned into service by the Metropolitan Transportation Authority, the station's landlord. Brody, the creative force behind much of New York City's postwar restaurant development, rose to the challenge.

The refurbished Grand Central Oyster Bar & Restaurant is one of America's most historic and celebrated seafood destinations. With its cavernous architecture and sweeping Guastavino-tiled ceilings, it

The Grand Central Oyster Bar
in New York City

is indeed a fitting cathedral to this remarkable bivalve. In 2014, the Guastavino tiled ceiling was completely renovated. The bar and restaurant received a James Beard Award in 2017 for Best Icon Design for a restaurant over 20 years old. And while it certainly isn't the only place in New York for oyster connoisseurs, it is the most spectacular. Just ask Patrick McMurray — we were delighted to have him guest-shuck at the Oyster Bar recently.

Women eating oysters at a bistro in France, circa 1950

IN PRAISE OF THE OYSTER

I'll never forget my first oyster. I was sixteen and a busboy at Beaujolais, one of Toronto's top restaurants. One night after service, Simon Bower, my restauranteur mentor, called me into the kitchen. "*Psst,* Paddy. Cover the kitchen door!" Simon whispered. "What for?" I asked. "Oysters!" he exclaimed. "Watch the front. Gerbil's got the back." After struggling with the shells, Simon proceeded to open a few oysters. He handed me one, nestled in its shell, and told me to slide it back. It was cold, sweet, and salty, like the ocean. I was hooked.

Except for the taste, I didn't know much more about these plump sea morsels until 1992, when I started at Rodney's Oyster House, a subterranean boîte on the lower east side of Toronto. On an average day, we'd shuck from twelve to twenty different types of oysters at Rodney's and, since the restaurant credo was "the oyster comes first," we had to know something about each one. Most of the patrons were satisfied if you told them where the oyster came from, but the more adventurous clientele were curious about how the oyster was grown and how it tasted.

One busy night as I was shucking at the bar, a customer asked me about the difference in flavor between a Malpeque and a Belon. I shot back, "Malpeque — salty-sweet. Belon — ocean sea salt, seaweed, and tin." With a laugh, the gent inquired, "Are you for real?!" But after he tasted the oysters side by side, without sauce, he understood what I meant.

The questions continued: How do oysters grow? Are wild oysters better than aquacultured ones? Do you ever cut yourself? What's the difference from one coastal variety to another? How can I tell if an oyster is bad?

Perhaps our fondness for oysters is ingrained in our DNA — an evolutionary throwback to our basic needs of water, salt, and protein. Upon first taste we cross over from "Ick! I will never eat that!" to euphoric moaning. We revel in the unseen pleasures of merroir — the taste of location on the palate that Mother Nature creates, the soft, silky texture of the morsel between the shells. The assembly of tastes — of light salt, ocean minerals with fresh vegetal flavors — sensations discovered only by crossing that line from desire to fulfilment, from curiosity to knowledge.

In 2001, I opened my first restaurant, Starfish Oyster Bed and Grill. We brought French and Irish Oysters to a local market known for classic Canadian shellfish. One of many questions that arose was

"How can the oysters be fresh, if they're from Europe?" To which I replied, "It's amazing what airplanes can do these days." It's only 24 hours from water to door in refrigerated transport from Ireland. It can take 36 to 48 hours for oysters to arrive from the Maritimes, depending on the weather, and traffic.

Olympia oysters: small in size but great in flavor — nature's *umami*

In 2009, I opened another restaurant, The Ceílí Cottage, an Irish local in Leslieville, in the east end of Toronto. We rebuilt a tired old car garage and infused it with the Ceílí soul of an 1880s slate-roofed cottage from the west of Ireland. One of the first questions a new patron asked me was "There are oysters in Ireland?"

"It's an island," I whispered to him, "ocean surrounds the place. In fact, you can find oysters anywhere in the world, wherever ocean touches land. Except Antarctica, but I haven't explored there … yet."

The oyster has been a cornerstone in our gastronomic history. With one simple tool — whether a shark's tooth or a thin, stone flake or rock — we can pick our shells and open a feast from the sea. Grab a knife, crack open the cover of this book, and take in the lore, history, and recipes, all the wonders of the oyster. I've been a-shucking 20 years and more, since 1992, and I am still learning: always ready to hear the next story, open a few shells, and taste what has come in from the latest tide.

I hope you enjoy *The Oyster Companion: A Shucker's Field Guide for Connoisseurs*. It is a book to take with you on your quest for the best oysters, to make notes, earmark, spill upon, and doodle in the corners.

Like our predecessors, taste, learn, evolve, and share the love.

Shuckingly yours,

Paddy

PATRICK McMURRAY
Toronto, Canada

Oyster seller and his traveling tricycle cart, Fujou, China

CHAPTER ONE

A SHORT HISTORY OF THE OYSTER

"It was a brave man that first ate an oyster."

JONATHAN SWIFT

Fossil records show that the oyster as we know it is about 25 million years old. The first *Homo sapiens* did not appear until roughly 200,000 years ago. So, who ate the first oyster, and why?

Imagine one Friday night roughly 500,000 years ago, *Homo erectus,* predecessor to *Homo sapiens,* accompanied by his elders, was walking along the shores of the place we know as Java. It's low tide after a storm and they discovered lots of sharp, shell-like "rocks" protruding from the sand — including some that had been smashed open. Our protagonist, the mighty *Homo erectus,* might even have noticed a bird or other sea creature snacking on an open shell. This curious sight, coupled with the oyster's invigorating scent, would have awakened a mighty hunger in our hunter. As he stepped into the oyster bed, he probably crushed a few fragile shells underfoot, exposing the flesh within. He reached down, and grabbed one for himself, plucking out some of the silky meat and experiencing its fresh saltiness in his mouth. It was a new flavor sensation — and a new source of easily acquired food. The hunter looked around, noticed that one of his elders had picked up a shark's tooth, jammed it into a shell, and pried it open to reveal another salty-sweet reward of the ocean. Our hunter continued to forage, gather, pry, open and eat. Oysters, clams, and mussels. Ever after, at low tide, he'd walk along the shore to feast. One day, content with a day's feed, our pre-person took the pry-tooth tool and scratched a little drawing into a shell. *Homo erectus* gave it to one of his elders — an homage to his teachings and to a good day spent shucking. A shucker was born!

Recent research by Leiden University uncovered a shell that was doodled upon some 500,000 years ago. It was a simple zigzag pattern, but a deliberate drawing done with, as speculated by professors, a shark's tooth. Shark's teeth would have been found across many if not all beaches. So it's not hard to imagine our *Homo erectus* hunter finding a tooth from a Megaladon shark and thinking, yes, this will work to pry open a shell.

Some theories state that early humans would have gathered near estuaries, where there was abundant forageable food and water supply. A stream that lead to the ocean would have been perfect for oysters and shellfish to grow naturally. Little did they know that by enjoying oysters, they were fulfilling their bodies' need for omega-3 fatty acids and zinc, helping to build healthy, stronger, and bigger brains. Sounds like eating shellfish could have had a hand in evolution.

Most early civilizations enjoyed the oyster in some form or another. Shell middens (mounds used as ancient kitchen scrap dumping grounds) have been found on every continent except Antarctica. Some of the largest and oldest on the East Coast of North America appeared along the Damariscotta River in Maine. The Whaleback midden at Glidden Point, Maine was formed over an estimated 1,000 years between 200 B.C. to A.D. 1000. The midden was used by several different tribes and is made primarily of oysters and other shells, and bones. At its peak, the Whaleback midden was more than 30 feet (9 m) deep, approximately 1,650 feet (503 m) in length, and between 1,320 to 1,650 feet wide (402 to 503 m). Throughout the late 1800s much of these shells were harvested for chicken feed, reducing the size of the midden, but this National Historic site is still one of the biggest middens in North America. That's a whole lot of shuckin' going on!

"The first man gets the oyster, the second man gets the shell" is a proverb that Andrew Carnegie (1835–1919), the American industrialist, supposedly enjoyed saying. Come late to the oyster party and you'll be staring at nothing but shells. It happens every time I'm shuckin' around catering gigs.

OYSTER PADDY.

Oyster Paddy postcard

19

Oyster farming first showed up in Asia around 300 B.C., moving larger oysters to secluded bays, and using stakes of bamboo, and wood, and rocks arranged in the water to collect spat when the oysters were milky, fertile, and spawning. Later, multiple rafts with floating concentrations of shells grown on strings and wire were moored and arranged in areas of great water supply, with replenishing tides to feed the oysters. Ancient Chinese drawings and paintings show these oyster farm arrangements were not much different from today's practice of oyster aquaculture.

Oysters were revered by the Roman emperors, who calculated their weight in gold and sent thousands of slaves to the shores of the English Channel to gather them. The Romans set up one of the earliest marine farms to keep a supply of oysters handy for their grand feasts. The silver coin "Denarius" was commonly used (A.D. 284–305) and was valued at one oyster, which would have been approximately a day's wage for a common laborer. Many Romans were familiar with the oyster's qualities — different varieties, tastes, and textures — and had preferences as to where the best came from. Roman poet Juvenal once described how a local epicure Montanus spoke of oysters:

> *"He, whether Circe's rock his oysters bore,*
> *Or Lucrine lake, or distant Richboro's shore,*
> *Knew at first sight."*

The Ancient Roman merchant Sergius Orata created some of the first oyster farms in the Mediterranean, and many of his ideas and practices are still used today. Orata was famous for his oysters that he "finished" in a different area than where they grew up. The volcanic, ocean-accessible Lake Lucrine, with its rich minerals and warmer water, caused oysters to fatten and refine their flavor. Orata's oyster farms used suspension methods of sacks, ropes, and sticks to hold the oysters off bottom, away from natural predators, silt, and sand. The raised oysters flourished in bountiful algae blooms for feeding. The layout of the "Ostriara" oyster ponds were drawn on several vases that have survived to this day (see one on display at the Corning Museum of Glass, Corning, New York) and depict the suspension methods, and even the warm-water basins built with fire chambers underneath, to keep the oysters warm during colder winters. Eventually, due to the popularity and lore that surrounded these oysters, the basin designs were later developed for hot spring Roman baths. What's good for the oysters is good for the people as well!

Europeans/French

Oyster eating continued throughout human history, and some of the concepts drawn up in ancient China and Rome are still in use today. The oyster farms of Marennes Oléron in France are a great example of taking *parc*, or ocean oysters, grown in linear suspension sack methods — like what was drawn on the vases centuries before them — and then finishing them in the high-tide ponds known as *claires*. *L'affinage en Claires* is essentially a method of force-feeding oysters, naturally, with algae, which is what they normally eat, while creating fat, plump foie gras-like ocean morsels.

Oyster farming on the Zuider Zee (Netherlands) ocean flats is difficult at best. But Dutch ingenuity in the 1700s brought the oysters inland, and today, companies like Smit & Smit are essentially farming oysters on land!

North America

When the Europeans started settling North America in the 1600s, they survived just as Native Americans did, by foraging. Oysters were definitely on the menu, and the appeal of natural oysters in the New World led to harvesting and cultivation using Old World farming practices. The oysters in North America were different than what the explorers were used to, hence the Latin name *Crassostrea virginica* was bestowed upon the shells. *Crassostrea* = cupped edible. *Virginica* = virgin. Virgin oysters.

Australia and New Zealand

Shell middens found around Australian coastal regions confirm that oyster eating has been going on for thousands of years in Indigenous culture. Oyster gathering and coastline farming using wooden sticks to hold the oysters until big enough was a common practice. Oysters were a valuable food source, and the shells were used as tools. It wasn't until the late 1800s that locals realized that stocks were being depleted from over-fishing, and farming practices were established in New South Wales. The French parc method didn't work well in the silty environment, but the suspension bag did and is still widely used today.

South Africa

In South Africa, both wild and cultivated oysters are consumed. Edible wild oysters include *Striostrea margaritacea, Saccostrea cucullata, Ostrea atherstonei*, and *Ostrea algoensis,* which all occur along the south and east coasts. These oysters are harvested commercially, recreationally, and via subsistence fishers.

Republic of Love

Speaking of rounding the Cape of Good Hope, oysters have long been regarded as aphrodisiacs. Robert Neild, in his delightful book *The English, The French, and The Oyster*, states that the most convincing explanation for this is psychological. According to Neild, people in primitive times in many parts of the world believed that shells had magical properties connected with fertility. These beliefs most likely originated with the first man who picked up a cowry shell on the shore and noticed that its shape, color, and form bore a remarkable resemblance to the sexual parts of a woman. Not difficult to understand, Neild points out, when you consider that two basic needs dominated the life of early man: the need to find food, and the need to perpetuate his race.

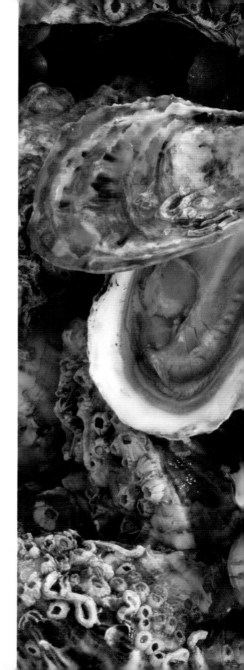

Speciales de Cancale oysters
from France

Mighty Aphrodite

With time, shells came to be viewed as symbols of womanhood, fertility, and birth among many primitive cultures, and they were often worn as ornaments or charms to enhance sexual potency and to ward off sterility. The scallop shell figures prominently in the mythologies of ancient Greece and Rome — including the myth of the birth of Aphrodite (to whom we owe the word "aphrodisiac"), who was carried to shore on a scallop shell after rising naked from the foam in the sea.

Fast-forward hundreds of years to my oyster bar in Toronto, and a completely different scene with Aphrodite unfolds. A young lady sitting at the bar and enjoying her oysters, plucks up the courage to ask me a burning question: "I've been told that oysters are aphrodisiacs. Is it true?"

"I haven't heard that before, please, do tell me more…" When the chuckles die down, I answer her question; an aphrodisiac can be anything that floats your boat. There are chemical and technical theories about the libido increasing over the effects of say, chocolate, too, but if you don't like chocolate, it's not going to work for you. That being said, Casanova reportedly ate fifty oysters a day while taking his morning bath, and one can only imagine how many Antony and Cleopatra consumed. Technically speaking, oysters are loaded with zinc, more than any other natural food source. Zinc helps to release testosterone in the body, both in males and females, which in turn drives the libido. The oyster is also very high in protein. The protein in oysters, however, starts to digest in the stomach, not in the gut. As the oyster digests and the proteins are broken down, you experience a burst of energy, a light euphoria which is yet another reason to start a meal with oysters: to keep you going through a big supper. Therefore, between digestion and chemical reactions, we have a stimulant — or aphrodisiac, if that's what you'd like to call it. Many oyster farmers have fun with naming their fare, and a favourite that comes to mind is the logo for Lucky Lime Oysters from Prince Edward Island: "Eat Oysters, Get Lucky."

The eyes tend to eat first, and an oyster can get very sexy in the right hands. A shucker places the blade close to the open palm. Grasping the shell, with forearms flexing and nimble fingers, often with blade on thumb, they guide the tip of the knife to the hidden hinge, the sweet spot. They gently insert the blade,

Charting an oyster's growth — from the end of its first year (top) to market size at the end of its eighth year (bottom). Drawings are not to scale.

careful not to bruise the soft flesh between the shells, to reveal the oyster within. All this is done within 4.2 seconds. To a shucker, four seconds is sexy, while normally being this fast won't get you very far.

Now, raise the shell to your mouth and smell the fresh ocean scent — sea breeze, salt, wet stone. A "mermaid's tear" of oyster liquor falls gently from the edge of the frilly shell, gracing your bottom lip, glistening. A breath. Slide the oyster from the shell, between your lips and onto your tongue. Two bites, nibbles really, gently bruise the oyster. Now aerate, breathe in through your mouth. The taste: salty, sweet cream, with a silky butter texture that caresses the palate as it glides to the back of the throat. The scent: like clean sheets tousled in an ocean breeze. The Pacific *Crassostrea gigas.* in particular, smells and tastes of cucumber. A few research papers have suggested that the scent and taste of cucumber can be an aphrodisiac for women. So between the fresh scent and the glistening oyster, it's easy to see that the libido kicks into gear.

Journalist and oyster lover Lisa Hilton writes of eating her first oyster: "It slipped down my throat as easy as original sin … and left me feeling mysteriously adult, sensually alive in a way I never had before, full of the promise of the future."

The next time that perfect plate of oysters comes to your table, pause to appreciate its beauty, then gaze into your partner's eyes for a few moments before you indulge.

AN OYSTER'S LIFE

During the summer, when the water warms up to the perfect temperature for each species, the oyster's gonads begin to swell in preparation for mating season. Males "spat out" sperm, females release eggs, and the two meet in the water to form microscopic zygotes.

Crassostrea oysters will spat out into the water and recover within a few weeks, so they can still be enjoyed at the bar year round. The female *Ostrea edulis*, meanwhile, fertilizes the eggs within her shell and keeps them inside from about May to August, when she releases them into the wild. This explains the old saying "Don't eat oysters in months without an R." I admit, though, I've been known to change my calendars to Mayr, Jrune, Jurly and Argust — when the great summer oysters arrive!

Well-groomed Wellfleet oysters in Chopper Young's hands, with seaweed

Once spat season is complete, the oyster parents are tired. After tending 300,000 babies at a time (a female may produce from 10 million to 100 million eggs a year), who can blame them? They may also be tired of being one gender and actually switch sex. This isn't much of a stretch, since most oysters have both male and female reproductive organs. Oysters are protandric; juvenile oysters usually mature as males first, then change to females later in life. Sequential hermaphroditism is the big word of the day — and I'd want to have a change of scenery if I'd "done it" 10 to 100 million times in a year, too!

The zygotes, meanwhile, float freely through the water column along with billions of plankton bits. At this point, the oyster is a food source for countless filter feeders, including other oysters. Barely one in a million will survive. They spend nearly a month drifting away from their birthplace, growing and changing as they begin to develop a shell.

When their shells are sturdy enough, the baby spat sink to the bottom wherever they happen to land. Each one extends a "foot" and moves along the bottom until it finds the perfect hard place to call home — perhaps a rock, a piece of wood, or another shell. Once it cements itself in place, it will continue to grow, feed, and reproduce in the same spot for years to come. By the end of three months, it's the size of a dime; by the end of a year, it's ready to reproduce.

For nourishment, the oyster filters water through its gills, extracting both oxygen and nutrients in the form of plankton. A 3-inch (7.5 cm) oyster can filter more than 3 gallons (11.4 L) of water every hour. This allows the creature to grow rapidly.

While the new babies fend for themselves, the parents concentrate on fattening up for winter. At this point, they're at their most succulent. From now until spring it's oyster season, an excuse for oyster festivals and competitions around the world. In the winter, when waters get too cold, oysters sensibly close up their shells, lower their metabolism rate to near zero and hibernate to save energy. This is called the "onset of quiescence." They can live off their stored fat and the liquor in their shell for weeks. In the spring, as the oysters "awaken." Their meat is so thin it's almost translucent. Then they resume feeding and putting on new shell in preparation for the mating cycle to begin anew. If the oyster is lucky enough to set in a bay that is warmer, without a winter per se, then that oyster will spend its time just eating (filtering), growing shell, and spawning. Oh, to be an oyster.

ANATOMICALLY CORRECT

If you enjoy oysters and are planning to open a few, it might be prudent to know a little anatomy.

The oyster is a bivalve with a two-part hinged shell. We call the left valve the top shell, or cap, and the right valve the bottom, or cup. A choice oyster will have a teardrop or rounded shape with a slight lean to the right from the hinge. The elastic hinge, located at the back of the oyster, keeps the shells open all the time in the water. Fine hairs called *cilla* run along the edges of the mantle and sweep captured food toward the mouth, located at the hinge. Opposite the hinge you'll find the lip, the best place from which to slide out the meat.

Remove the top shell and you'll see the mantle, the thin membrane surrounding the body of the oyster. It's responsible for excreting nacre, a liquid form of mother of pearl that creates an oyster's shell from the inside out. A layer of new shell is exuded several times a year, each layer no thicker than tissue paper. As this malleable material hardens, it forms another layer on the oyster's shell.

Nacre is also responsible for creating pearls when a piece of grit enters the oyster.

The adductor muscle, which makes oysters so difficult to open, is located two-thirds of the way up from the hinge. As it contracts, it pulls both shells together against the force of the hinge. This muscle is made up of fast-twitch (dense, opaque, and white) and slow-twitch (more translucent beige) muscle bundles. The percentage of each will determine how long an oyster can stay out of water. *C. virginica*, with more slow-twitch, can last a month out of water, while fast-twitch oysters such as *Ostrea edulis* will only last a week.

Between the mantle, four sets of gills help extract oxygen and food from the water. You'll also notice the stomach, usually filled with greenish algae and plankton. Just behind the adductor muscle sits the heart valve, which pumps liquor around the oyster through the circulatory system at the base of the gills.

A MATTER OF TASTE

Many people think that oysters are bottom feeders and, therefore, somehow unclean. This is false. Though wild oysters can be found on the ocean bottom and quite often attach themselves to rocks, piers, and other hard objects, they do not feed from the bottom. Instead, they're filter feeders, which means they filter plankton and algae directly from the water. Oysters are persnickety — choosing what to consume — and transferring that to the stomach, all else is left in the ocean.

You may recall plankton from science class — microscopic organisms that drift with the tide and provide food for other creatures. Phytoplankton are marine plant life near the surface, while zooplankton are animal life, and feed on other plankton and the larvae of fish, and crustaceans floating 16 to 33 feet (5 to 10 m) deep. To take advantage of both types of feed, oyster farmers keep oysters at various depths. In this way, even oysters grown in the same bay will taste different.

Oysters that have grazed in the photoplankton zone produce a more vegetal finish, sweet with hints of melon, cucumber and lettuce, while those from the zooplankton zone deliver a more steely finish, clean, light and crisp.

Another indicator of taste is the type of water oysters are grown in. Oysters need fresh (sweet) water, and the percentage of salt to sweet affects the meat's flavor and texture. Oysters grown in saltier bays will have a brighter flavor, while those grown in "brackish" water, with its high percentage of fresh water, will taste slightly salty up front with a milder finish.

Nature's perfect food — and eco-friendly, too!

Over the years, people have often asked me about the nutritional content of oysters. I always think of them as a delicious food that brings you in contact with the sea, but the oyster is also one of Mother Nature's most perfect foods. In fact, it's so packed with nutrients, it's no wonder most people experience a protein-induced buzz after eating a number of oysters.

- Oysters are high in omega-3 fatty acids and low in cholesterol. They're an excellent source of vitamins A, B1, B2, B3, C, and D, and are loaded with minerals such as iron, magnesium, calcium, selenium, and zinc. They're also a good source of easily digested protein. A 100-gram serving of raw *C. gigas* oyster meat contains 73 calories and just 2 grams of fat; 100-gram serving of *C. virginica* contains 60 calories and 1.5 grams of fat — perfect for health-conscious diners who are watching their figures.

- Oyster farmers don't feed or add any chemicals to their crop. Instead, they keep the oysters in an area where they can grow and be fed by Mother Nature.

- Oyster farming, or aquaculture, is a sustainable resource that helps keep the environment healthy. As oysters snack on plankton, they help keep its growth in check. An overabundance of plankton clouds the water's surface and prevents nourishing sunlight from reaching the aquatic wildlife below. (Just think of oysters as environmental heroes!)

- Far less energy input is required to produce an ounce of protein from an oyster than most any other protein source. Beans to beef, oyster (and cultured filter-feeding shellfish) trumps all. No feed, antibiotics, water, energy/electricity needed to grow, and little fuel is required to harvest (depending on how far from land the oyster is grown). Save the ocean (*ahem*, the world), eat an oyster!

At the bar, I try not to say that oysters are a healthy food, good for you as well as the environment — as that type of image ruins the oyster's sexy, late-night aphrodisiac qualities — a real shuckin' PR nightmare.

Leslie Hardy's crew grading on the beach, Ellerslie, Prince Edward Island

TO GROW AN OYSTER

Edible oysters grow naturally near the coast or on banks farther off shore where the water temperature is right and the sea bottom firm. They do particularly well in estuaries, where seawater mixed with sweet water nourishes the growth of the types of plankton that suit them.

Our ancestors originally gathered oysters by picking them up full-grown on the shore at low tide or by lifting them from natural beds at sea. In Europe, the coarse, cheap oysters of the mid-nineteenth century were a product of that kind of fishing, but they were fished out. A natural supply of mature oysters is rare in Europe nowadays.

In countries such as England, Ireland, and France, oyster cultivation consists of two stages: obtaining young oysters, and tending them as they grow and fatten.

According to Neild's *The English, The French, and The Oyster*, there are two traditional methods of obtaining young oysters: by dredging a natural bed for spat and part-grown oysters; and by collecting on a private bed any spat that formed when larvae drifted in from natural beds or from private beds nearby. Once young oysters are ½ inch or more in size, they are known as brood and are bought and sold for laying down to grow and fatten.

The key to the breeding of oysters, whether on public or private beds, is to have enough breeding stock in a suitable place and to maximize the area of sheltered clean, hard surfaces on which larvae can settle to form spat. The traditional method of doing this is to provide a

hard bed of "cultch" — a mixture of the old shells of oysters, cockles, mussels, and other shellfish, plus other suitable oddments, such as bits of broken crockery, and ceramic roofing tiles. In the middle of the nineteenth century, manufactured surfaces, or "collectors," were introduced in France (a Roman practice rediscovered).

Before the spatting season, the bed needs to be raked to remove weeds and to lift existing cultch out of the mud, and new cultch needs to be added. Artificial collectors have to be prepared and put out.

The oyster grower needs to watch over the oysters regularly to make sure they are not smothered by silt, sand, or weed; damaged by predators, pests, or competitors for space and nutrients; or stolen.

Colville Bay oysters in bags, on trestles, and full of promise

Oyster laying, both for breeding and for later growth, may be on the foreshore (the area between high and low tide), or farther out to sea. With a laying on the shore, the oyster farmer needs to ensure that the oysters are covered in seawater all or most of the time while still enabling himself to tend them on foot.

Where the shore is relatively flat, an oyster grower can enclose an area above the normal low-tide level so that it will retain a few inches of water while the tide is out. Such enclosures are called *parcs* in France.

Oyster beds farther out have to be tended from a boat with dredges and harrows. The aim of dredging is to skim off oysters, cultch, and rubbish. What is brought up is sorted. Rubbish will be removed and oysters thrown back until they are ready to be harvested as brood or for consumption.

Before oysters are marketed, they may be moved into areas where conditions are ideal for fattening them and for maximizing their flavor. In some parts of France, a complex system of artificial beds, called *claires*, has long been in use for this purpose. Claires are shallow basins with clay walls located in marshy areas at the level of high tide. Water is let into them at high spring tides and retained by a system of dykes and sluices until the next spring tide. In the summer, the stagnant water in the claires develops a bloom of blue-green organisms that tinges the oysters a greenish color — an indicator to the consumer that these are among the most flavorful of bivalves. Claires were first introduced at Marennes, which at one time was a major source of flat oysters and was renowned for its seasonal supply of Marennes vertes.

An oyster farmer at a saltwater claire in France

OYSTERS IN THE BAG

Amédée Savoie and Maurice Daigle, the owners of La Maison BeauSoleil in New Brunswick, on the East Coast of Canada, place their oysters in mesh Vexar bags suspended from long lines until mature, without being finished on the bottom — an interesting variation on a practice that dates back to Roman times. This labor-intensive approach produces a consistent Cocktail oyster with a meat-to-shell ratio greater than any other oyster on the market. It's always full and plump, with a lovely salty-sweet taste and steely, clean finish.

WILD IN GALWAY

Galway oysters are one of the few true wild oysters that I know of. Apparently, local folks tried to aquaculture the *O. edulis*, with limited success. So they returned to their original methods of stewardship. When the beds start getting thin, they're closed to harvesting for up to five years so the oysters can grow and replenish the stock. When the beds reopen, the oldest oyster can weigh more than 200 grams. If you happen to know the grower personally, some of these gems might just end up in your order (thanks Dairmuid and Michael!).

Michael Kelly, of Kelly Shellfish, has a grow-out lease of 800 acres in Inner Galway Bay, which is fed from the fresh runoff of the fields of Athenry and flushed by cold Atlantic waters. This magical combination creates one of the world's most distinctive oysters, available only from September to April. The oysters are finished over 10 acres in Killeenaran, Clarenbridge. "The Fields of Athenry" is a well-known song everyone sings with tear in their eyes while dancing on chairs at the Oyster Festival. It's a Galwegian thing.

The family has six full-time and six seasonal employees who together harvest some 200,000 oysters a year. Mature oysters are dredged out of the Inner Bay and rest in the finishing area for a number of days or weeks. To harvest them, the Kellys simply walk out at low tide and gently lift the oysters into a waiting basket with the help of a stiff rake or pitchfork. The harvested oysters are taken back to the farm for cleaning, culling, and grading. They're then loosely arranged in trays of 100 and returned to the water to rest again. "The oyster doesn't like to be brought out, then boxed and shipped," Mr. Kelly Sr. told me one year. "Too much shock to their system. Better to let them rest for a couple of days, then they'll travel better."

Tide coming in on the Kelly beds, Galway Bay

OYSTERING À LA CARTE

Foraging for your own seafood by the sea is an unforgettable experience. It's also easy, if you know what you're doing and you do your homework in advance.

No matter where you go, even if you have land with a water view, call the local Fisheries office to make sure the area you are harvesting in is in good condition. They'll be able to tell you what shellfish is available in that area and what the limits are.

You'll need a pair of rubber boots, a bucket, an oyster knife, and some gloves. Oyster shells can be sharp, especially in warm weather. The boots will keep you from cutting your feet, which is not fun.

Head to the area at low tide and pick up oysters as you walk along the beach. Quite often, you'll find a group attached to rocks or other objects. Just take the knife, pry a few off, and put them in the bucket. Make sure you test a few, of course, to ensure they taste good.

When your bucket is full, take your oysters home and rinse them under cold water. If they are muddy, a little scrub brush will help.

You can serve the oysters at "ocean" temperature, as you found them, which provides the best flavor. To chill them before shucking, make a bath of ice and water and let the oysters sit in it for 20 minutes.

After your feast, return the shells to the area in which you found them to give spat a good place to set.

Buckets in hand, young children search for oysters in Port Notre Dame,
Ile de Re, France

CHAPTER TWO

THE BIG FIVE

"Oysters spend their lives — dozens of years if we left them alone,
but only three or four because we don't — sucking in seawater,
extracting nutrients [from it] and pumping it out again…
And perhaps this is why oysters taste like eating the sea."

MARK KURLANSKY, *The Big Oyster*

So many oysters, so little time … so where to begin? When the neophyte oyster lover sits at the bar, the choices can be overwhelming, even more so than when choosing a wine. An oyster's flavor is based on 1) species, 2) location, 3) finishing — season/weekly weather patterns, and/or claire pool finishing. Oyster bars, though able to bring in a large variety of species at all times of year, will stock their menu with the best of the season.

Always ask the shucker what he or she recommends, then set a parameter, if you have one. East only, West, or anything goes. No matter where you go, I suggest starting with a dozen oysters: six types, with two of each, so that you can pick your favorites and then have more of what you like.

If you are fortunate enough to find an oyster bar that offers all five species, you can have a "flight" of oysters as a tasting. Ask the shucker to arrange the oysters in ascending order of flavor, beginning with the delicate Olympia and ending with the metallic tang of the European Flat. And please, no sauce or lemon to obscure the true flavor of the ocean. Oystering for the first time is an awakening, ocean molecules embedded in our DNA, calling us back to the water, like a siren's enchanting song. We are all drawn to the ocean, and luckily the oyster brings the ocean to us.

Like terroir in the wine world, the merroir (or sense of place in the ocean) of the oyster will denote the specific flavor within that family. Salty, sweet, freshwater, earthy notes, all will change from place to place. That's what makes the oyster so exciting as a food. There is nothing quite as complex in its simplicity as an oyster, and it can take you back to the sea in one quick sip. The oyster is a snapshot of the location from where it came, and the day it was plucked from the sea. No other food can transport you more easily to a location via taste. Close your eyes, open your mind, and let the oyster take you there.

Dignitaries sample local bivalves at the Duchy of Cornwall Oyster Farm during the first Cornwall Oyster Feast, 1925

JUDGING THE TASTE OF OYSTERS

There are three elements to the taste of an oyster — salinity, texture, and pure taste. And all are influenced by the waters from which the oyster comes. Local waters each have their own characteristics, and these change from day to day and from season to season, depending on the temperature and the amount of rainfall (which alters the supply of freshwater).

The salinity of most favorable oysters should be neither so high that it makes the oyster sharply salty, nor so low that it makes it insipid. The texture should be firm, not milky or stringy. Mother Nature wins, and dictates to what the oyster will taste like for the most part. Pending your palate, all of these tastes will be observed in the oyster — favorable or not.

As for the taste… That's a much harder thing to describe. I like the phrase John Neild suggests: *le goût de la mer* (the taste of the sea). It's a simple description, and one that an oyster lover will immediately understand. We'll talk more about the taste of oysters in a minute (see Tasting Wheel, page 50). Now, let's look at the oysters themselves.

Five species are regularly shucked in North America: *Crassostrea virginica, Crassostrea gigas, Crassostrea sikaema, Ostrea edulis,* and *Ostrea lurida.* Within those species are a myriad of different oysters that can be enjoyed at oyster bars wherever you go.

Oysters representing the five species: (1) *C. gigas* — Marina's Top Drawer, Canadian West Coast; (2) *C. virginica* — Colville Bay, P.E.I., (3) *O. lurida* — Olympia, Washington State; (4) *C. sikaema* — Kumamoto, Wahington State; and (5) *O. edulis* — Kelly's Galway Flat, Ireland

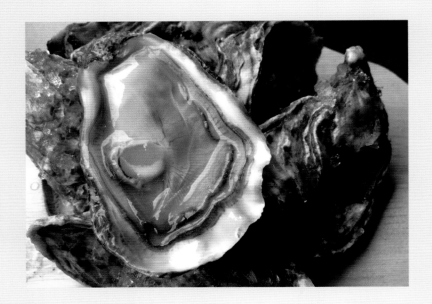

PATRICK'S TASTING WHEEL

As I've said, oyster tasting is a lot like wine tasting. I recommend that you chew your oyster a little bit, two bites, and aerate (take in a little air through the mouth) to allow the flavors to cross the palate and develop fully. I've been describing oysters like wine for years now. People are amazed when I tell them how the oyster they're about to enjoy will taste, and when. As with everything from nature, flavors will change throughout the season and according to location. So go forth, young oyster connoisseur, and open your palate to the bounty of the sea. Just don't top your oyster with sauce first!

Top: Kelly's Clarenbridge Bay (*C. gigas*) Rock oyster
Right: Patrick's Tasting Wheel: for oyster aficionados and sommeliers alike

START → SOFT/COOL SALTS

HOT SALTS

MID-RANGE

FINISH

TEXTURE — MOUTH-FEEL

plump, firm, meaty, crisp, chewy, silky, thin, watery, mealy

Wheel labels (inner to outer):

FINISH · NOSE · UPFRONT · BODY

WATER · SALT · FLORAL · SPICE · FRUIT · VEGETATION · NUT · WOOD · MILD · EARTH · SWEET · METAL · CLEAN · FAULTS · MICRO · SULFUR · BIOTIC · DRY (TANNIN) · STRONG · MEDIUM · LIGHT

WATER: bland · neutral (sweet/freshwater) · brackish · soft · seabreeze · salty · brine · iodine

SALT: ocean wave · astringent · geranium · seabreeze/seaweed · alstroemeria · anise — licorice

FLORAL / SPICE / FRUIT: white pepper · lemon/grapefruit · apple · cantaloupe · honeydew · watermelon · melon rind · cucumber · bell pepper · lettuce · fresh-cut grass · herbs · seaweed

CITRUS · TREE · MELON

NUT / WOOD / VEGETATION: cashew · walnut · green sap wood · driftwood · straw · rich butter · sweet cream · forest floor · mushroom · leather · potting soil · ocean mud · silt

SWEET: white sugar · corn syrup · brown sugar · stainless steel · iron · tin · copper · bronze · brass · horsey · sweaty · sour — lactic acid · sulfury — egg · sulfitic — match, rubber · sulfidic — sewage, gas

CRASSOSTREA VIRGINICA

Yes, I know it's a mouthful. *Crassostrea viginica* is North America's favorite species. Known widely and more commonly as the Atlantic or East Coast oyster, its round to teardrop shape, smooth, hard shell, and well-defined hinge makes this oyster a dream to shuck.

In taste, *C. virginica* is generally a perfect balance of salt and sweet but will range in intensity depending on its birthplace. I find that oysters from colder, more northerly waters tend to have a brighter, more briny flavor, while southern oysters tend to have a milder, sweet fresh flavor, and their plump texture makes them ideal for cooking.

C. virginica can take anywhere from 18 months, two to three, and up to seven years to reach market size of 3 inches (7.5 cm) for a small Choice. Larger oysters, sold as X/L Fancy grade, have been known to be eight to 12 years old. The latest trend is to grow a Cocktail grade oyster of just under 3 inches (7.5 cm). Customers tend to enjoy the smaller size and price, while growers get a faster return on their investment.

These popular bivalves are found naturally in the ocean's intertidal zone — the part of the shore that's submerged at high tide and exposed at low tide — where they live in a mixture of salty and sweet (fresh) water to a depth of 40 feet (12.2 m). Eastern oysters are being grown from the cold water of New Brunswick all the way down to the tip of Florida and around the Gulf of Mexico. You'll even find one or two of them on the West Coast these days.

Amédée Savoie flips over some float bags of his Beausoleil oysters

Hundreds of growers produce many different varieties within this species. Many are grouped under regional names, each with its own unique flavor: Malpeque, Blue Point, Maine, New England, Chesapeake Bay, Apalachicola, and Gulf oysters. And the best oyster bars distinguish varieties by grower as well as by location.

No matter where you go on the ocean, the locals will always say that they have the best oysters in the world. And in a sense, they all do. Let's take a quick tour of some of my favorites.

Malpeque Oysters

To the uninitiated, a Malpeque is any oyster from Canada. Malpeques derive their name from the largest bay on the north shore of Prince Edward Island. Technically, any oyster from P.E.I. can be called a

Malpeque but, even within the province, there are great differences among the oysters. (In 1898, the Malpeque oyster won gold at the World's Fair in Paris and everyone on the Island has used the name Malpeque ever since!) In taste, the Malpeques strike a perfect balance between salty and sweet.

Cascumpec Bay Oysters
Cascumpec Bay, Prince Edward Island

Distinctively brown, smooth shells give the impression that these oysters are rack-grown and tumbled with the tide to create perfectly shaped shells every time. The brown coloration comes from the minerals in the local peat bog, and a wonderfully light salty-sweet earthiness comes through in the flavor and texture of Casumpec Bay Oysters.

Measuring an Atlantic oyster — the extension in the culling hammer marks the legal size of 3 inches (7.5 cm)

Colville Bay Oysters
Souris, Prince Edward Island

Johnny Flynn started in the oyster business in 1993, after the cod fishery dried up along the East Coast of Canada. Since then, he's been growing some of the best oysters in the country, thanks to the ideal conditions of the waters around Souris (a winning combination of depth and algae growth). Johnny uses a French Table System to grow his oysters in the shallows of the Souris River for the first two years, then spreads them on the floor of the bay for the final two years. Colville Bay oysters, with their signature green shells, are an even teardrop shape and range in size from 3 to 3.5 inches (7.5 to 8.9 cm).

Johnny doesn't like to cook his oysters: "Too nice on the half to take the heat." I once had him ship me some green crabs, the oyster-eating blighters that had been infesting the oyster beds of P.E.I. and still are. Martha, the chef at my previous restaurant, Starfish, made a wonderful crab bisque and, at the last moment, poached a few Colville Bay oysters and floated them on top of the chowder for good measure.

The texture of the Colville's are second to none on P.E.I., matched only by the historically interesting Grand Entrée from the Magdalen Islands. Interestingly, the ferry to the Magdalen Islands docks at Souris Harbour — the same bay that Colville Bay Oysters are grown. My theory is that oyster seed from the Magdalens was scooped up into the bilge water tanks of the ferry and deposited in Souris, where they met up with the local Malpeques in Johnny Flynn's backyard and eventually created the fantastic Colville Bay Oyster we see today. Look for them at Adam Colquhoun's Oyster Boy in Toronto and several other lucky venues among his wholesale customers.

Colville Bay oysters — the greener, the better!

Oyster racks in Colville Bay — note the red silt on the water's bottom

Hardy's Malpeques
Ellerslie, Prince Edward Island

Owner and oyster grower Leslie Hardy incorporates bed transfer methods, buying oysters from independent harvesters and spreading the stock across his beds for finishing in the crystal-clear waters of Malpeque Bay. These are the quintessential Malpeque — and the quality of the meat, the briny-sweet taste, and the excellent value make this one of the most popular oysters that I shucked at Starfish and still do today at The Ceílí Cottage.

Green Gables — Single Bed Oysters
New London Bay, Prince Edward Island

George Dowdle grows a fantastic "sugar snap pea" oyster in New London Bay, P.E.I. The Green Gables oysters are rack-grown from seed to finish after four to five years of residing on George's salty oyster bed, which is sweetened by four spring water wells that bubble up under the tidal zone. The Daffodil Oyster is a hand-graded prefect Green Gable, offered through Seacore Seafood in Toronto as a fund-raising initiative for Canadian Cancer Society research. Eat a Daffodil in support of a good cause and #ShuckCancer!

The Raspberry Point Oyster Company

The Raspberry Point Oyster Company grows six different brands of oysters around P.E.I., employing several different growing methods to establish the varietals. Raspberry Point, Irish Point, Pickle Point, Daisy Bay, Shiny Sea, and Lucky Limes are each distinct and first rate. Grower James Power's remarkable over-wintering technique ensures great oysters all year long. "All that and a bag of chips!" James Power is also adept at butter, cheese, and ice cream production with Cows Ice Cream of P.E.I. Oysters to ice cream — perfection.

Winters can be quite heavy in P.E.I., so all summer the crew squirrels away 10,000 count racks of graded oysters into the middle of New London Bay. In mid-winter, when the orders come in, James will drive out to the marked site of a rack and, using his trusty 6 feet (185 cm) chainsaw blade, will cut through the ice and raise 10,000 oysters at a time for the happy and warm city folk waiting at their local oyster bars. On behalf of city folk everywhere, we thank you hearty souls, plucking oysters from the frozen sea.

ROD — Rodney's Oyster Depot
Nine Mile Creek, Prince Edward Island

Rodney Clark, the "Bishop of Bivalves" himself, has his own oyster beds along the South Shore of P.E.I. in a wonderful location where his oysters fatten and finish to salty-sweet plump perfection. "Like a D size, in a B cup," as Clark is oft heard bantering across the bar. Prince, Queen, and King oysters named for the counties of P.E.I., can be found exclusively at Rodney's Oyster Houses across Canada.

Rodney Clark, oyster purveyor, grower, impresario

NOT JUST ANOTHER MALPEQUE

BeauSoleil Oysters
Néguac, New Brunswick

Amédée Savoie, vice-president and general manager of La Maison BeauSoleil, has a background in fisheries management and worked with the Department of Fisheries and Oceans before founding BeauSoleil Oysters with partner Maurice Daigle in 1999. The company cultivates approximately 10 million oysters a year, using some of the most advanced methods in Canada. (Savoie and Daigle are often spotted in France, scouting new ideas for oyster growth.) Off-bottom growth is done in the shallow waters of Néguac Bay using long-line float Vexar bags. The men have mastered a technique that cements oysters to a rope, then suspends them off the bottom on custom racks. This allows for faster growth, since the oysters are not overcrowded. An oyster harvested this way is known as the French Kiss.

BeauSoleil oysters are harvested after five years and are graded using an ingenious photo-imaging machine that takes a photo of each oyster, analyzes it in a computer, grades it, and moves it down the conveyor belt to the appropriate box — at a rate of one oyster every two seconds! BeauSoleil's in-house lab inspects every batch of oysters for meat density as well as water quality. If the meat-to-shell ratio is below standard, the oysters are sent back to bed for a little fattening up.

While the BeauSoleil shell may look smaller than most other East Coast oysters, the amount of meat in the shell is the same,

or greater. These petite aquacultured oysters have a medium saltiness and a sweet, steely, clean finish, thanks to the cold northern waters that they call home.

In winter, Amédée drives a truck across the frozen bay, then chainsaws a hole in the ice so that he can harvest the well-placed lines of oysters (see photos). The trick is to do this quickly because, at -22°F (-30°C), the oysters will freeze rapidly once they're out of the water. At this time of year, the surface ice concentrates the salinity of the bay, making the BeauSoleil oysters saltier than usual.

Pristine Bay Oysters
New Glasgow, Nova Scotia

The waters off the northern shore of Pictou County, Nova Scotia, are said to be pristinely clean, hence the name of these hand-grown oysters. Thanks to the high percentage of fresh water that enters this bay, the oysters have a uniquely mild flavor, more sweet than salt.

Pristine Bay oysters are also one of the easiest oysters to open. In 2002, I won a place in the *Guinness World Records* for opening 33 oysters in one minute, using cold November Aspy Bay, N.S. oysters. I broke that record in 2010 in Beijing, but in 2017 Gordon Ramsay called me out for a *Guinness Records* head-to-head challenge. I took Pristine Bay oysters to Los Angeles and laid out 39 oysters in 1 minute, just barely squeaking past the chef of Hell's Kitchen (full story, embellished across the bar nightly at 7:35 p.m. at the Ceílí). To my mind, Nova Scotia has some of the fastest-shucking oysters in the world, due to their hard, deep shells and wide-open hinges, and Pristine Bay oysters are right there on top.

Taylor Shellfish Farms — West Coast Virgins
Shelton, Washington State

This is a special treat if you are fortunate enough to find it. While the *C. virginica* oyster is indigenous to the East Coast of North America, a number of Pacific growers, including Taylor Shellfish Farms in Washington, successfully grow this non-native oyster species.

West Coast Virgins, as I call them, offer the best of both worlds: the salty-sweetness of the East, with a suggestion of the West in the melon-and-cucumber finish. A firm texture and hard shell make this oyster a shucker's dream.

Grand Entrée
Magdalen Islands, Quebec

Good luck finding this one. It's the last bastion of one of the most perfect East Coast oysters I've ever tasted.

As an experimental project of the Quebec government in the 1970s and early 1980s, local seed stock was reared and grown for a while, then abandoned after it was noted that the oysters took too long to reach market size. Years later, in the late 1990s, an enterprising fisherman brought some of these oysters to Toronto and sold them to Rodney's. They were so good that we probably depleted the existing stock. I am hard-pressed to find one today, although I continue to believe (wishful thinking?) that there must still be a small number of oysters there, since I remember noticing yearling oyster shells on the larger ones that arrived in Toronto. Hope springs eternal.

The shell of the Grand Entrée is very thick and hard from years of slow growth, perfectly shaped, with the most amazing color of Kelly green on the outside. The meat, "button-tufted" like a pillow, was fat and plump, the color a dark, creamy beige. A salty, crisp bite into the meat revealed the perfect, sugar-sweet finish. I miss them so, but can find a close likeness in the Colville Bays of P.E.I. Although the Grand Entrée have not resurfaced, Trésor du Large oysters are cultured in the Magdalens today.

NEW YORK'S BLUE POINT OYSTERS

Think Blue Point, think oysters grown and served in the New York area. The oysters cultivated in Oyster Bay, New York, are bottom-grown and are the definitive East Coast Blue Points. Sweet and salt up front; firm, plump, and meaty texture, with a buttery, woody finish. They are often covered in limpets, and I find that the more limpets attached, the better the oyster meat within. The limpet knows all!

A true Blue Point has an appellation. Similar oysters are grown from Long Island, Connecticut, New Jersey, to Virginia. The name Blue Point was so popular in the 1800s that fishmongers and harvesters would use the title to sell their oysters. In 1908, N.Y. legislature passed a law stating that True Blue Point oysters must have been cultivated in the water of the Great South Bay, Long Island. This law was never really enforced, and there is only one grower today with the True Blue Points — Blue Island Oyster Farm, at Fire Island. Luckily, Chris ships all through Manhattan, Long Island, and across the country.

THE OYSTERS OF MAINE

There is something magical about the waters of Maine. Everything seems to taste sweeter and cleaner, from the fish to the lobsters (and, of course, the blueberry pie). The oysters from Maine are no exception, with a sweetness reminiscent of sugar cubes!

Pemaquid Oysters
Dodge Cove Marine Farm, Newcastle

The Pemaquid is an oyster-bar classic: plucked from the waters of the Damariscotta River and infused with a sweetness you won't find anywhere else. Three to six inches (7.5 to 15 cm) long, with a hard, obsidian-like shell and a plump, meaty texture, this oyster opens with a sweet salt brine and finishes with a sugary-sweet snap. Invigorating, and definitely worth sampling.

Glidden Point Oysters
Edgecomb

Barbara Scully, founder of the Edgecomb Point Oysters, knows her way around oysters. With a background in marine biology, she believes in — and practices — a sustainable method of oyster growth, with no overcrowding of bags and beds. The result? A perfect teardrop shape, the envy of the *virginica* crowd, for the company's signature Glidden Point oysters. Generally deep-cupped, the shells are very hard, and therefore easy to open. The meat is plump, toothsome, and firm, with a bright ocean sea salt and a beautiful sugar-sweet finish.

When the orders come in, Glidden Point divers dive to the floor to hand-harvest the oysters. This method is not only easy on the fragile oyster but also great for the surrounding environment. The company website (gliddenpoint.com) is also worth a visit.

THE OYSTERS OF NEW ENGLAND

Harvested along the coast of Massachusetts, New England oysters are crisp in texture and are fat and plump. There is a salty sweetness to their taste, as there is with Malpeques, but there is also an underlying note of earthy seaweed.

Cotuit Oysters
Cotuit

Located in the heart of Cotuit Bay, the Cotuit Oyster Company has been producing its world-famous briny-tasting oysters since 1857. Owner and oyster-grower Dick Nelson starts his oysters from seeds the size of a grain of sand. The seeds are contained in special floating hatcheries (a floating upweller system, or FLUPSY) where they can be accessed and tended until they grow large enough to be bed-planted for their final grow-out. This deep-cupped East Coaster is another oyster-bar classic. It is best enjoyed raw, but its plump, meaty texture also holds up well to the heat of cooking.

Welfleet oysters in an Australian mesh tube

Wellfleet Oysters
Cape Cod

Chopper Young is a world champion oyster shucker (Galway, 2008) whose operation is as back-to-basics as you can get. He brings in oysters from the public beds and allows them to grow in a small plot of water across from the harbor. As the tide moves out and the oyster bed is exposed, he can (literally!) drive out to his oysters to tend them. Since the oysters are market grade, Chop can bag them right there on the lift gate of his pickup, then take them either to the co-op wholesaler or right to market in Provincetown (the Lobster Trap is a big customer). From water to restaurant in 15 minutes. Now that's fresh!

In 2007, Chop and partner Allison Paine (a seventeenth-generation "Caper") installed some of her father's "Australian" oyster long-line Seapa grow-bags and have improved the number and quality of the oysters, as well as the time it takes to grow them.

You'll know a Wellfleet by its sea-salt taste and a plump, crisp, meaty texture that gives way to a nutty, earthy, sweet finish.

THE RETURN OF THE CHESAPEAKE OYSTER

At one time the largest oyster-producing area in North America, the waters of Chesapeake Bay suffered from massive overfishing and from over-industrialization of the area. Oysters are now being farmed here. More hands-on harvesting, racks, long lines, and tumbling create these fantastic half shells. They are mild, more sweet than salty, wonderfully plump, and meaty — perfect in any recipe that calls for cooked or half-shell oysters. Rappahannock, Hollywood Oysters, and Shooting Point are houses of note.

Gulf Coast Oysters

Like the Malpeque, the Gulf Coast oyster is an umbrella name for almost every bivalve plucked from the Gulf of Mexico. Since the Gulf waters are a lot warmer than the waters of the Atlantic coast, the oysters are mild-tasting but plumper and meatier than any other oyster in North America — and great for cooking. This is the home of the fried oyster, po' boy sandwich, and Oysters Rockefeller (not to mention the oyster bar's ubiquitous Tabasco sauce).

Apalachicola Oysters
Florida

The mainstay of Panhandle oyster bars, this firm and meaty beauty grows to market size in just 6 months! (Since the water is so warm, there is no hibernation period.) Just be wary in the summer months, when it may get too warm for oystering.

Murder Point
Alabama

This family-run oyster operation uses an Australian grow-out method of long-line Seapa Oyster Baskets to allow easy access to the oysters, and a natural, vigorous tidal tumbling. This tumbling creates a perfect, smooth, deep teardrop cup to house the plump, buttery-sweet salt oyster they call #Butterlove. One of the few oyster farmers in the Gulf, they labor and love the oyster into many oyster bars. Try them at Alabama's own establishments.

Keeping warm-water oysters fresh

- **AmeriPure** has a patented process for cleaning and flash-pasteurizing Gulf Coast oysters. The oysters are harvested, culled, and scraped and the shells high-pressure cleaned. Then they are banded and dipped, first in hot water, then in an ice-water bath, to "shock-kill" any harmful bacteria. The band ensures that the oyster remains closed during the entire process, retaining all its natural flavor and liquor. The oyster is not cooked but remains fresh in the shell, and has a greater shelf life than its unprocessed counterparts. This is a great way to guarantee the freshness — and the safety — of warm-water oysters.

- **Hydrostatic High Pressure (HHP)** technology is used in processing Gold Band Oysters from Louisiana. Once the oysters — about 60 pounds (27 kg) at a time — are put in the customized pressurizer and surrounded by water, the pressure is increased to 80,000 pounds per square inch! Because the oysters are submerged, the pressure is equal on all sides. This effectively crushes bacteria, killing them off. The pressure also causes the oyster's adductor muscle to detach from the shell, leaving the oyster perfectly "shucked" in the shell. Once the oysters emerge from the 6-minute-long process, all it takes is a light touch on the shell to open it. For the half-shell market, the oysters are "banded" with a shrink-wrap band to keep the shells closed during processing.

Six minutes, 60 pounds, 99 percent bacteria-free — makes me dizzy! Good thing these machines can't talk, make jokes, or mix drinks. Or can they?!

The distinct — and distinctly beautiful —
shells of *Crassostrea gigas* and *Ostrea edulis*

CRASSOSTREA GIGAS

Originally from the Pacific Rim, *C. gigas* is now known as the number-one oyster grown around the world. Because this oyster can be grown and sold year-round and matures in just two to four years, it has become a grower's favorite. It comes in various shapes and sizes, depending on whether it's raised in the water on racks or on the beach.

An elegant and frilly-shelled *C. gigas*, basking in Pacific light

On the West Coast of North America deep fjords cut by the glaciers of the last ice age leave virtually no room to allow bottom or off-bottom aquaculture, so growers suspend trays off the ocean floor on long-lines or rafts. As the oysters mature, the growing trays are moved to different depths so the bivalves can graze on different types of plankton, which changes their flavor. Rack-grown oysters tend to be smaller in stature, round to oval, with paper-thin shells ending in elegant flutes and frills in black and white.

These creatures may be beautiful, but shucking them is a challenge — like trying to hold a sackful of razors. Some rack growers tumble the oysters regularly to break off the frills and coax the oysters to produce a thicker shell so they're easier to transport to market and to shuck.

Rack oysters tend to have a more vegetal finish, reminiscent of melon or cucumber. In North America, we know *C. gigas* as a Pacific, or West Coast, or Gigas oyster. In Europe, it's marketed as a Rock oyster, to distinguish it from the native (or Flat) oyster.

Pacific *C. gigas* oysters have a naturally occurring cucumbery scent and flavor. Did I mention that cucumber is thought to be an aphrodisiac for women? The scent and taste, that is, so bonus aphrodisiac qualities in a Pacific oyster is all I'm sayin'.

OYSTERS FROM CANADA'S WEST COAST

Royal Courtesan Oysters
Cortes Island, British Columbia

Brent "The Oysterman" Petkau hand picks these Pacific oysters on a tide-swept beach on Cortes Island once they reach maturity and delivers them directly to homes and restaurants. Dark-mantled, between 3 and 6 inches (7.5 and 15 cm) in size, with a rounded cup and cap, the Royal Courtesan is a very plump, meaty oyster with beautiful notes of cucumber and melon.

Effingham Bay
Barkley Sound, British Columbia

This is as west as you can get on Vancouver Island, British Columbia. The remote location is not easy to get to, but it's easy to appreciate the clean, deep, cool Pacific waters that create Effingham Bay oysters. Sweet and buttery up front, the salt is mild and clean in the finish.

Mac's Oysters
Fanny Bay, British Columbia

Shucked pints and gallons, from the larch beach ands cluster oysters — handy for cooking without the shells. Mac's carries half-shell deep water oysters like the soft and melony Pearl Bay, and Sinku, Beach Hardened Buckley Bay, and Ship's Point.

Out Landish Shellfish
Heriot Bay, British Columbia

Desolation Sound and Denman Island have a great flush of tidal waters that bring in nutrients and keep the water moving around the variety of oysters and shellfish that grow at Out Landish. Beach Angels are hardened on the beach, which naturally thickens the shell and adds a light earthy flavor to the oyster. Marina's Top Drawer is just that, grown up at the top of the water, to encourage heavy feeding and frilly shell growth.

WASHINGTON STATE OYSTERS

Taylor Shellfish Farms
with locations in Seattle, Shelton, and Samish Bay

In my mind, no other group in North America grows as many oysters — four of the five North American species, including the rare Olympia, and rarer still Virginica (East Coast oyster grown on the West Coast) — in as many locations as Taylor Shellfish (Samish Bay, Totten Inlet, and Willapa Bay are just a few). Shigoku and

Fat Bastard are Taylor's signature oysters, tumbled smooth, with flavors of soft sea salt, and butter melon. These Pacific oysters grace the tables of many oyster bars across North America.

Willapa Bay Oysters
Willapa Bay

Protected from the rugged Pacific by a natural sandbar, Willapa Bay is situated just north of Oregon along the Pacific Coast. Its shallow waters are sweetened by spring water running in from the surrounding coastal range, which adds a wonderful touch of earth and seaweed to its namesake bivalves. The deep-cupped Willapa Bay oyster is just over 4 inches (10 cm) long and almost 3 inches (7.5 cm) wide, with deep fluting and a creamy-colored shell. The cream-colored meat is plump and crunchy-firm.

Workers harvest oysters buried in the muddy bottom of Willapa Bay

OYSTERS FROM CALIFORNIA

Hog Island Oysters
Tomales Bay

The Hog Island Oyster Company grows its oysters in the waters of Tomales Bay, a narrow, 22-mile-long (35 km) inlet fed by the Pacific Ocean. Part of the Gulf of the Farallones National Marine Sanctuary and bordered by the Point Reyes National Seashore, the bay's shallow waters and rich plankton blooms provide a perfect place to grow the signature Hog Island Sweetwater — a plump oyster with a light salt up front and an appealing creamy texture.

MEXICO

Kumiai Oyster
Baja, Mexico

I know what you are thinking: Mexican oysters? Open your mind; Kumiai oysters are fantastically complex and briny. Get ready for salt as well as plump umami from the shores of the Pacific side of Baja. These shells can be found at the farm or at any of expert shucker/ chef Drew Deckman's restaurants. Grab your passport — it's worth a trip south.

ACROSS THE ATLANTIC

Let's pause for a moment while I tell you the story of how *C. gigas* arrived in France and became Europe's adopted oyster of choice. Once upon a time, France's original native oyster was called the *punt*, and this is the oyster the Romans found so delightful. It has been described as round and flat, with a taste of metal or iodine. Sounds like a present-day Belon, doesn't it?

The *punt* grew alone on the Atlantic shores of France until 1868, when a ship carrying Portuguese oysters (*Crassostrea angulata*) was forced to dump its cargo in the Girade estuary during a storm. *C. angulata* flourished in the nutrient-rich waters and by 1922 had overtaken the native punt (which had been decimated by a gill disease epidemic).

The Portuguese oyster, unlike the *punt*, was highly prized for its plump sweetness. In 1967, another blight wiped out 80 percent of the oyster stock in France and threatened the future of the oyster as the centerpiece of Christmas celebrations. A proposal was put forward to restock France's oyster beds with a hardier strain of the *Crassostrea* family — the *gigas,* or Japanese oyster. The original stock came from Canada's West Coast, where *C. gigas* had been aquacultured since the early 1900s to meet the local demand for oysters after the collapse of the native Olympia.

C. gigas proved to be a very hardy creature indeed, and easier to grow than the native species. Other countries soon followed suit, in the wake of overfishing and industrial pollution that drove native species to near-extinction. Today, *C. gigas* can be found nearly everywhere oysters are grown in Europe. And around the world, for that matter.

VIVE LES HUÎTRES!

No one, I think, is more passionate about oysters than the French. They have been harvesting them since before the Romans came for a "visit." There are two main types grown in France: the *Ostrea edulis* (the native Flat) and the *Crassostrea gigas*. Within *C. gigas*, the French have developed a classification system that is so refined, it can be a little confusing; but once you understand how it works, you will know exactly what you are getting when you order your oysters.

There are over 3,400 growers in France, each with a different idea of how to cultivate and to "finish" their oyster. Some just grow and harvest in oyster parcs; others like to finish their oysters by holding them in brackish water ponds or pools called *claires*. (see page 22). Accordingly, the two main types of *C. gigas* served in France are Parc oysters (which include the small and affordable Creuses, the larger Longues, and the shapely Fines) and Claires. The four types of Claires all attest to a level of quality in taste and are strictly regulated in the marketplace.

A proper Parisian seafood tower, done just right

Fines de Claire, Fines De Claire Vert, Spéciales, Pousse en Claire
France

The first time I came across this green-frilled oyster, I thought to myself, "Hmmm … you don't see that every day. This will either kill me or it will be the greatest oyster ever!" As luck would have it, I discovered one of the most intensely flavorful bivalves the sea has to offer. And it all has to do with algae.

With a cream-colored shell, algae-green highlights and fine frills on the outside, the shell of a Fine de Claire is often chalky and brittle, so shuckers beware. The meat inside is what is the most interesting. A proper Fine de Claire should sport a green gill — tinted that telltale shade when the algae diatoms that the oyster is feeding on get caught up in the gilling. And the taste is a burst of bright ocean sea salt, seaweed and vegetal sweetness.

This oyster is often shucked with the top mantle removed or, better still, folded over to show the green gill petit fours. *Oh, la la!*

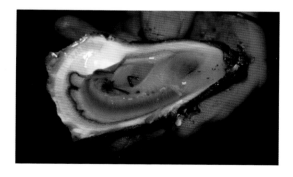

A Malpeque with gills gone green with algae, mantle removed

IRELAND

Kelly Oysters
Killeenaran, Galway Bay

This is a classic West Ireland oyster: full, plump with sweet cream and buttery, light seaweed notes. One of my favorite summertime oysters, packed in a wicker basket with local seaweed — it's hard to top.

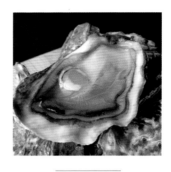

Kelly's Clarenbridge Bay
(*C.gigas*) Rock oyster

Harty Oysters
Dungarvan Bay

On the East coast of Ireland and the Celtic Sea, the nutrient-rich bay creates such a good oyster that French growers are moving in to get first crack at great shells. Harty Oysters are that perfectly plump, buttery, salty-sweet and slightly seaweed-vegetal-finish oyster you'd expect from well-groomed shellfishers.

Achill Oysters
Achill Island

Cold and remote waters make for delightfully oceany oysters. These are a rare find, but should be sought out while in Ireland.

Dundrum Bay Oysters
County Down

Northern Ireland's Oyster Grower and Shucking Champion Robert Graham grows lovely bright and light *C.gigas* oysters.

GERMANY

Sylter Royal Oysters
List on Sylt, Germany

Germany's only oyster farm grows using off-bottom trestles on the mud flats of the North Frisian Islands. Sylter oysters feature a hard shell and briny, green vegetal earthy notes.

PORTUGAL

Moinho dos ilhéus
Sitio dos Ilhéus

Grown in well-protected ponds off the Atlantic Ocean, these *C. gigas* oysters are tumbled smooth and have a wonderfully briny taste. Find them at Restaurante Barbatana in Lisbon.

MOROCCO

Huîtres Kandy
Dakhla Bay, Morocco

These oysters are actually grown where the Sahara Desert meets the Atlantic Ocean. Huîtres Kandy grows *C.gigas* oysters from seed to market in 15 months off sandy beach shores.

SOUTH AFRICA

South Africa is home to a range of oysters from the Ostreidae (True oyster) range. There you can find the Weed oyster (*Ostrea algoensis*); the Red oyster (*Ostrea atherstonei*); the Natal rock oyster (*Saccostrea cuccullata*); the Cape rock oyster (*Striostrea margaritacea)*. Also common in these waters are saddle oysters or Anomiidae. They are not harvested for food consumption (not very tasty) but rather for industrial uses like paint and glue.

Famous in the region but also not edible are the Cape Pearl Oyster (*Pinctada capensis)* with their mother of pearl interior shell.

Saldanha Bay Oyster Company
Saldanha Bay, South Africa

A company that is as engaged with sustainability as they are growing, they offer a wide range of *C. gigas*. From spat to market, cocktail oysters of 40 grams to 50 grams are ready in 8 to 10 months. Medium-size oysters of 60 grams to 70 grams take 10 to 12 months, large oysters between 80 grams and 90 grams have a grow-out period of 12 to 14 months, and extra-large oysters, weighing 90 grams to 110 grams, take 14 to 16 months to become market-ready. Giant 1 oysters of between 110 grams and 130 grams take 16 to 18 months, while Giant 2 oysters take 18 to 20 months to mature to between 130 grams and 150 grams.

UNITED ARAB EMIRATES

Dibba Bay Oysters
Gulf of Oman

Pacific *C. gigas* grown in the northern Fujairah emirate started from a pilot project in 2014 whose aim was to see if oysters could be cultivated in the azure waters of the Gulf of Oman. In 2017 Dibba Bay produced their first ever harvest. These oysters can be found at Traiteur restaurant in the Park Hyatt Dubai.

UKRAINE

Skifian Oyster
Black Sea, Odessa Region

Skifia's oysters are grown on the Black Sea coast in the Odessa province in southern Ukraine, near the Tuzly Lagoons National Nature Park. Skifian Oyster is the first oyster farm in mainland Ukraine. Its name refers to Scythia, the ancient Greek name for the northern coast of the Black Sea and beyond. The owners hope to return Ukraine to its place in the 1880s, when it was a world-famous oyster exporter.

JAPAN

The Kakiemon oyster is available year-round due to the cool, temperate waters of Hokkiado. They are firm and plump, and taste slightly creamy/buttery with a cool cucumber finish.

SINGAPORE

Seafarmers @Ubin

Seafarmers @Ubin are growing Pacific *C. gigas* oysters and can deliver from sea to table in the same day, anywhere in Singapore.

AUSTRALIA

Home to a range of oysters including the Pacific oyster *(Crassostrea gigas)*, the Sydney rock oyster *(Saccostrea glomerata)* the Angasi (flat) oyster *(Ostrea angasi)*, the Milky oyster *(Sacostrea cucullata)* and the Blacklip oyster *(Striostria mytiloides)*. The Pacific oyster is native to Japan with current production concentrated in China and the United States. Sydney rock oysters and Angasi oysters are native to Australia, and their shells have been found in ancient Aboriginal middens.

NEW ZEALAND

Home to Pacific oysters (*Crassostrea gigas*), New Zealand also has Bluff oysters (*Ostrea chilensis*) and Rock oysters (*Saccostrea commercialis*).

Coromandel Oyster Company
Coromandel, New Zealand

These *C. gigas* are gorgeous and plump, with pale creamy meats and black lashes. A minerally oyster from New Zealand. Great shell structure, frilly, and well packaged for travel all the way to North America!

CRASSOSTREA SIKAEMA

The rare West Coast Kumamoto oyster is harvested by only two or three growers that I know of, yet it's fast becoming a household name. These miniature, flavor-packed creatures were brought to North America in the 1920s from Japan's Kumamoto prefecture, where over-fishing later led to their near-extinction. Take a look at a wonderful documentary *Ebb and Flow* by Shelly Solomon that celebrates the Japanese-American Yamashita family's work.

Kumamotos are small — at most, 2 inches (5 cm) long. They have a rounded slight teardrop shape with a surprisingly deep cup; some are almost as deep as they are long. A classic Kumo (see below) will have a flat cap and a deeply fluted cup that resembles a cat's paw when turned upside down. It may look difficult to open, but the relatively hard shell and wide hinge actually make it fairly easy to shuck.

The Kumamoto is grown in Washington State, Oregon, and Southern California's Baja Peninsula. But the best, in my opinion, are a pure-bred Kumo grown by Taylor Shellfish Farms in Puget Sound, owned by Bill Taylor, one of the largest oyster growers I know and one of the few to produce all five species.

The Kumo's salty taste up front ranges from mild to briny, depending on the weather that week and other environmental factors. On the whole, however, it's mildly salty with a sweet, creamy texture and a hint of melon and cucumber in the finish. The meat inside the deep cup is also surprisingly plump, with a slight, toothsome firmness. These factors make the Kumamoto the second-most-requested oyster at my oyster bar, just behind Malpeques.

OSTREA EDULIS

O. edulis is better known as the European Flat, as you'd guess, because of its flat appearance. You may also find it called a Belon — although, like Champagne, this tender, sweet oyster should only be called Belon when it originates in Brittany, France.

Wild Flats grow naturally from Scandinavia to the Mediterranean. In North America, they're aquacultured in Maine, New Brunswick, Nova Scotia on the East Coast, and British Columbia and Washington State on the West.

O. edulis is round with a very flat top. The bottom can range from flat to a very deep cup, depending on its age and how it was grown. I find that aquacultured *edulis* tend to be flatter and shallower in the cup than their wild cousins, with a meatier texture.

Flats were once the choice of kings, queens, and emperors alike. Wonderfully complex in flavor, their popularity dates back to Roman

O. edulis Loch Ryan, Scotland's only native oyster

times and gave rise to the earliest forms of aquaculture. They're also technically difficult to open — which explains why Flats (Irish Flats, in particular) are the oyster of choice at the Worlds and other European Oyster Opening Championships.

If you're sampling various oysters, I suggest you sample an *O. edulis* last, to allow your palate to adjust to the intense flavors — sea salt up front, with sweet and earthy seaweed tones, then a metallic tang of tin, brass, and copper in the finish. Like the tannins in red wine, it's an oceany experience.

Glidden Flats
Maine (USA)

The flat oyster is not native to North America. A batch of *O. edulis* were brought over to the United States in the mid-1940s as an experiment to see if they would grow here. Lo and behold, it worked — but the Flats took five to seven years to make a market-grade oyster, and the tinny, or tannic, more complex flavor was "off-putting" to the market at the time, so the project was cancelled. Years later, *O. edulis* was showing up in local catches of Eastern oysters, and it has been deemed that a wild set of *O. edulis* was naturalizing itself in the magical Maine waters.

Today you can find Maine Belons in only the most selective oyster bars — there's not a lot to go around, and as *edulis* does, they run a short season due to the reproductive cycle (May to August — months without an *R* — sound familiar? This oyster adheres to that rule.)

Banded Glidden Flats

Belon Oysters
France

Grown where the River Belon meets the Atlantic in Brittany, this is one of the most intense and complex oysters around. Smell the soft, salty sea breeze in the nose, revel in the crisp cream and slight earthiness in the taste and enjoy the dry, metallic finish. Take in a little air to experience the full flavor. Keep an eye out when opening, as the thin, chalky shell can be brittle at times.

Kelly's Galway Flats
Galway, Ireland

When you hear the saying "Guinness and oysters," this is the oyster folks are talking about. The hard shell ranges in size from 3.5 to 5 inches (9 to 13 cm), with a very deep cup and slightly rounded top. You may notice thin pockets of nacre where seawater has been caught in the shell, but they won't harm the meat. The taste is rustic and real, with the scent of Irish air — fresh, clean salt and seaweed. And that's just the nose. On the palate, expect bright sea salt, seaweed, sweet cream and driftwood with a dry, metallic finish. Don't forget your pint! Moran's Oyster Cottage, just outside Galway (see Chapter Five), transforms these Flats into their reputation-making garlic oysters. Well worth the price of a ticket to Ireland.

The Netherlands

The Dutch oyster fisheries are located in the North Sea coastal region of the Eastern Scheldt and Lake Grevelingen. About 30 companies and individuals are active in these fisheries, Smit & Smit among them, which coordinate nearly the whole supply of Dutch oysters ranging from *C. gigas* to the *O. edulis* Dutch Imperial oyster.

Tio Point Oysters
Blenheim, New Zealand

Going back in the industry for 35 years, Tio Point Oysters is owned by two families who have cultivated mussels and oysters over nine farms. These native flats are related to the Belon in shape, structure, and taste.

New Brunswick Flats
Canada

This rare find is grown in an inland, saltwater lake on the south shore of New Brunswick. The shell is quite large, chalky, and finely layered, so approach it with caution. The meat is medium salty with a crisp, toothsome texture and bold, dry, brassy finish. One family has these oysters in a saltwater lake off southern New Brunswick. Not readily available at the moment, the good folks of La Maison BeauSoleil are aiming to get the flats to market — hopefully sooner than later.

OSTREA LURIDA

The Olympia oyster, named after the Olympic Mountains of Puget Sound in Washington State, is the only oyster indigenous to North America's West Coast. It's also one of the smallest oysters, reaching a whopping 1 inch (2.5 cm) in four years.

Despite its small stature, the Olympia has the biggest and most complex flavor of any oyster. This is a thinking man's oyster, to be eaten without condiments. In fact, I flat out refuse people in The Ceílí Cottage if they request lemon, sauce, salt, or pepper. Nothing but your lips — the flavors are too delicate to mingle with external forces.

A classic Oly tastes of sea salt to start, sweet cream, seaweed, earth and fresh-cut grass — a taste unique among oysters. Its dry metallic or tannic finish will last for up to 15 minutes, if you let it. To enjoy it fully, I suggest you look at the shell, ponder its existence, and hold the oyster in your mouth for a moment to let its silky texture caress your tongue. Next, draw in a little air, as you would when tasting wine, to let the flavor reveal itself fully.

Though it was once prevalent from California to British Columbia, overfishing and human industry have depleted the Oly to near-extinction. Today it's grown only in Puget Sound and Oregon but I've heard from British Columbia that Olys are moving back north. Stay tuned.

The Olympia Oyster Company has been rearing the petite Oly since the 1800s. In the early 1900s, cement embankments were placed below

The mighty little Olympia oyster, beloved the world over, is making a comeback

the waterline to create stepped growing areas. These embankments were back-filled with gravel to create a hard surface for the oysters to grow on. As the water recedes with the tide, the embankments fill with water, allowing the oysters to continue feeding and the grower to tend his beds.

CHAPTER THREE

FROM SEA TO TABLE

A treatise to oysters, penned long ago by an English monk about the local Ostrea edulis, *states: "Do not eat oysters in months that do not contain the letter R in the spelling [May, June, July, and August]."*

Most people I know can recite this saying, and many more still abide by it. If it were absolutely true, however, I'd have to shut down my oyster business for 4 months of the year. The rule originated in the days before reliable refrigeration, when oysters couldn't be transported to market in hot weather without spoiling quickly. Today, with proper management and plentiful stocks, oysters can be shipped around the world in refrigerated boats, trucks, and planes — which means you can find great oysters all year long. The species of oyster and where it's harvested determine whether you can eat a particular variety.

But there is definitely some truth to the *R* rule, as M.F.K. Fisher reminds us in *Consider the Oyster:* May, June, July and August are the months when the waters are warmest almost everywhere along the coasts, and the 70°F (21°C) temperatures are ideal for oysters to breed their spawn. Which brings us back to our English monk's edict:

A cluster of wild-growth oysters

the only species of oyster today that continues to be "offline" from May to September is, in fact, the *Ostrea edulis*. The female keeps up to 30 million eggs in its gills from about May until August, making the oyster meat "silty" and not very palatable.

In North America, the two predominant oyster species, *Crassostrea virginica* and *Crassostrea gigas*, release their spat into the water. The oyster's meat becomes creamy before spat, then very thin and translucent. This silky, sweet-cream texture is very different from the oyster's texture the rest of the year. Some customers appreciate it; others find it off-putting. Within three to six weeks, however, the oyster returns to restaurant-grade quality.

A summertime, milky *C.gigas* oyster, when shucked properly, can be used to make a delicious oyster and steak tartare — replacing the egg yolk with oyster "yolk."

Since reproduction takes place in warmer waters, northern oysters are available when southern oysters are reproducing. As the cycle moves up the coast, southern oysters become available while their northern cousins reproduce. I change my buying practices based on the various reproductive seasons, north to south and east to west. From about October to May, I sell a full range of oyster varieties, but I can source delicious oysters year-round.

Ostrea edulis oysters aside, the next time you hear someone invoke the *R* rule, you might want to consider M.F.K. Fisher's advice: "People who have broken the rule and been able to buy oysters in the forbidden months say that they are most delicious then, full and flavorsome.

They should be served colder than in winter, and eaten at the far end of a stifling day, in an almost empty chophouse, with a thin cold Alsatian wine to float them down … and with them disappear the taste of carbon dioxide and sweaty clerks from the streets outside, so that even July in a big city seems for a time to be a most beautiful month."

The Oyster Stand, Nicolino Calyo, circa 1840 –1844

STAYIN' ALIVE...

Different oysters will stay alive out of the water from one to four weeks, depending on the species, how they're grown, and how they're transported. With the shell sealed tight by the adductor muscle, the oyster inside can survive on its own liquor. Refrigerate it and it will curl up and hibernate, dropping its metabolism to a bare minimum as it does in winter. This is how oysters can survive a long trip to market. If the muscle is damaged or the shell gets chipped, however, the seal will break and allow the liquor to leak out, causing the meat to deteriorate.

Under optimal conditions, *C. virginica* will survive up to four weeks out of water, especially if they're wild and have endured the constant exposure to tides. *O. edulis,* including Irish Wilds, will last three weeks or more. Rack-grown oysters, with their thinner, more delicate shell, will survive two to three weeks. *C. gigas* and *C. sikaema* oysters will last two weeks. Belons, with their thin shells, must be eaten within a week or two, while the sensitive *O. lurida,* the Olympias, require extra-special care and won't last more than a week.

Some *edulis* growers "band" their oysters before shipping, to keep the adductor muscle from expending too much energy. It's a nice touch, and it extends the oyster's shelf life.

At the Ceíli Cottage, I buy only what I need for the next few days. Overnight shipping allows me to rotate my stock often, and I'd rather run out of one type of oyster than have an oversupply. Trust your oyster wholesaler!

BUYING OYSTERS

In the absence of a local oyster bar, a fishmonger or wholesaler who specializes in fresh fish is the next best place to find a quality oyster or several different varieties. They may even shuck them for you and provide them cap-on for parties. (If you cannot find one, e-mail me and I'll try to help out: paddy@shuckerpaddy.com.)

Most large grocery chains carry some shellfish in their fish department, especially in the winter months. Some will shuck the oyster if you're using the meat for cooking or chowder, but don't count on it. The best part of the supermarket experience is its buying power — you may just find oysters at the best price around.

Baskets of oysters for sale in Trouville, in Normandy, France

Then there's IQF (Individually Quick Frozen). This technique freezes food fast to help keep it fresher, longer. Some oyster growers have successfully experimented with this process, selling frozen oysters on the half for cooking, with the sauce already prepared. Freezing oysters on the half-shell does change their consistency and flavor somewhat, but if you're having 150 people over and toss them on the grill, nobody will be the wiser.

The internet offers one of the best ways to find unusual and wonderful oysters from all over the world. If the reviews sound promising, I will contact the grower and place a small order so I can see how it performs in my restaurant. If an oyster doesn't travel well, there's no point in buying it. You could also ask your local fishmonger to arrange a shipment for you.

Oysters at Blackpool Beach, England, 1942

SIZE MATTERS IN NORTH AMERICA

Just as there are many types of oysters, there are also many ways to buy and sell them. It can be confusing even for me, as I need to remember how each supplier likes to grade and ship. *Grade* refers to the oyster's size and shape.

Choice: the easiest to open and the best-looking oyster on the half-shell. A classic shape is the teardrop with a deep cup, flat to convex top with a clean shell. These command the highest price.

Standard: more of an elongated oval with odd angles and thinner shells. It's not as pretty, but the meat within will be just as good as the Choice oyster it grew up beside. Medium-priced, it can be served on the half-shell at big parties, or cooked into chowder or other dishes. We often train new shuckers on Standards because it's cheaper and because, if you get good at shucking Standards, shucking Choice oysters is a piece of cake.

Commercial: are often clustered together, making them difficult to shuck. These ugly ducklings are used primarily for the canners or shucking plants.

Some growers will pack 10 dozen per bag or box for easy counting. In Europe, the size is determined by the weight of the individual oyster. In North America, East Coast oysters are sold as Cocktail (2.5 inches/6 cm), Small (3 inches/7.5 cm), Medium (3.5 to 4 inches/ 8.75 to 10 cm), Large (4 to 5 inches/10 to 12.5 cm), and Extra-large, Jumbo, or Fancy (6 inches/15 cm and up).

STORING OYSTERS

Fresh bivalves should always be stored on ice or in a refrigerated cooler. Never keep them for a long time in water, which will kill them. If buying for home, place oysters in a stainless-steel bowl or pan, cover with a cold, damp cloth, and store at the bottom of the fridge. If the shells are open, they should close when tapped. Most importantly, the oysters should smell like clean ocean sea salt. If there's an unhappy smell of sulfur or fermented leaves, take a pass.

I store my oysters in their original container until I need them. A covering of silt, mud, or seaweed is a natural way to keep oysters happy and can be washed off just before shucking. But most of the oysters I receive are cleaned by the grower before packing.

If an oyster is particularly silted or dirty, I'll spray the dirt off in the sink, making sure not to plug the drain with sand. If you buy oysters in Styrofoam, plastic, or mesh bags, it's best to wash them off and transfer them, cup down, to a stainless-steel bowl or pan. This keeps them moist in their own liquor. Cover with a clean wet towel so the shells won't dry out, then store them on the bottom shelf of the fridge.

If you want your oysters to be ice-cold when you serve them, place them in an ice bath (half ice, half cold water) for 15 minutes, like Champagne.

HOW TO SHUCK AN OYSTER

There are two facts I like to keep in mind whenever I begin shucking.

First, at the 2006 World Oyster Opening Championship in Galway, Irishman Michael Moran beat contestants from 17 other countries by opening 30 oysters in 2 minutes 35 seconds. It was Ireland's first win in 10 years. But Michael could not get close to the spectacular record set by his father in the 1970s: 1 minute and 31 seconds!

Second, France produces roughly 130,000 tons of oysters annually, largely Pacific. The French consume more than 90 percent of those oysters themselves — raw, on the half-shell. Most oysters are consumed between Christmas and New Year's Eve. Common injuries requiring medical attention reported during that season are a champagne cork to the eye and a knife to the hand.

Fair Warning: If you are going to shuck, you will get cut — eventually. It may not be from the knife, it may come from the sharp shells, just know that this may occur. Protect yourself; pay attention as you are pointing a knife tip directly at your hands. "Keep your eyes on the oyster" is always my motto.

OYSTER SHUCKING TECHNIQUES

Even if you'll be shucking only a few times a year, it's worth investing in a sturdy oyster knife. I've heard too many stories of people injuring themselves while trying to open oysters with a screwdriver. (And don't even think of using a kitchen knife.) An oyster knife also makes a great screwdriver and a fine opener for letters, paint cans, beer bottles, and boxes. It will even un-lock doors and windows, so I've been told. Every kitchen should have one.

You'll need a sturdy board with a damp cloth beneath to keep it from slipping — an old chef's trick. The board can be as simple as a piece of 2 x 4 inches (5 x 10 cm) wood. Starfish shucker Lawrence David cast his "board" in cement, using a pie plate as a mold, with half a tennis ball in the center to create a shallow depression. Even a hockey puck makes a great non-slip shucking surface. My latest design from Swissmar is just that — a wooden Shuckin' Puck raised on a stainless-steel tray. Just what's needed for shuckin' around.

To protect your hand, you can invest in a glove (see Chapter 6). Or you can use a tea towel (but choose one that you do not mind getting oystery). The technique is simple, but it works beautifully.

First dampen the cloth, then fold it in half, four times, to create a small square. Place the folded cloth on a board, with the folded side toward you and the last crease to your left hand. Once you're ready to start shucking, place your left hand (or right, depending on which hand you are more comfortable holding a knife), on top of the cloth. With your thumb, open up the cloth all of the way and place an oyster inside, hinge pointing out toward you. Now cover the oyster and hold it in place for shucking. You should hold the oyster firmly enough so that it does not move. In this position, the cloth acts like a protective glove, but eight layers thick! No knife will be able to penetrate the cloth; even so, be careful and go slowly.

Now we're ready to begin. (Have you washed your hands? Remember, cleanliness is next to oysterliness.) To set up your station, position the board in front of you, preferably in a tray to keep the area clean. Pile un-shucked oysters to your right (if you are right-handed), place a second tray above the board to collect the top shells, and place a third tray, filled with crushed ice, to your left for the fresh-shucked oysters.

The oyster generally has a teardrop shape, which points to where you should be opening — a slight gap in the shells where it is hinged with collagen to keep the oyster open when in water. The hinge is the strongest part of the shell, so if you enter the oyster here, less shell will break or chip into the meat. The hinge is where you will make the cleanest of shucked oysters.

All shells are not created equal — round, flat, deep oval, soft shell, new shell layers are all factors that will determine which way you shuck. The hinge is the area that all species, and shapes, can be shucked open.

Most people will slurp their oyster from the lip or bill. There is a micro-thin opening, and if you enter the oyster from this angle, the shell generally chips off, so you have to sweep that out of the meat after. Some shuckers using this method will serve the oyster on the top shell, revealing a plumper-looking oyster, with less oyster liquor. The French believe that the true liquor comes from within the oyster, and the rest is just seawater and should be tipped out before eating.

The side opening is closest to the adductor muscle, so with the right technique, and oyster shell, shucking this way can be quick and clean. This is a classic French technique and the matching French oyster knives (for example, Leguille) will work best. The blade must have a thin kerf, but not too thin or the blade itself will break.

Step 1: Holding the oyster tightly (with the cup side on the board, and the hinge pointing to your wrist), insert the tip of the knife into the hinge, the pointed end, and work it deep into the hinge with a slight twisting motion, as if you were twisting a key in a lock. Don't force the knife into the oyster; you're merely introducing metal to shell. Once the knife is set into the shell, give it a quick twist and you should hear a pop or snap as the hinge breaks.

Step 2: Using your free forefinger, pry up the top shell to the point where you can peek inside and see where the adductor muscle is attached. Using your knife, scrape this area, and the top shell will come off. Pay attention, though, as most shuckers will remove the top mantle from the oyster as it sticks to the top shell. Place this shell in the tray in front of you. (Some of these shells will come in handy for presentation.)

For hinge shucking, hold tight (*above*); point, pry and peek (*below*)

Step 3: To free the oyster from its bottom shell, turn the shell 180 degrees so the adductor muscle — the dark "button" in the flesh — is closer to your knife. If you're left-handed, you won't need to turn the shell. Scrape just under this muscle and free the meat. (If the meat is still stuck at the hinge for no apparent reason, you've just discovered the remains of a second adductor muscle that oysters possessed at one time million of years ago.) Touch the flesh gently and you'll feel it release. Once you've loosened the meat from the bottom shell, sweep it gently with your finger to remove any grit or shell bits.

Scrape at the adductor muscle to release top shell

Step 4: With your free hand, place the oyster onto the presentation tray. Then with your other hand, reach for your next oyster.

Place your shucked oyster nicely and keep going!

ONE IN THE HAND

This technique is most effective in small spaces, on a boat, in a canoe, or just plain walkin' around. It's also quick and easy. At the same time, it's riskier for amateurs and requires your full attention. You'll need a knife and a cloth or glove. A stainless-steel mesh glove is the only glove to protect yout hand from a stabbing. On my last trip to the Worlds, I knifed my finger in exactly the same place I'd injured it four years earlier, almost to the day. As I pulled out the knife, it "strummed" across the tendons. Luckily, I still have a full range of motion, but my finger was a little numb for a while. I now use a mesh glove with the fingers cut off.

North American shuckers generally "stab" through the hinge, away from the hand, then clean off the top and bottom.

French shuckers, meanwhile, use a side-entrance technique, inserting their knife into the side closest to the adductor muscle, severing the top of the muscle and removing the top shell. They don't sever the muscle completely (except in competition), for historical reasons. In the late 1800s and early 1900s, oysters in France were served on special ceramic plates with deep indents for the shucked oysters. This allowed people to eat their oysters with a fork, without touching the dirty shells. Unfortunately, some chefs started replacing the fresh oysters with tinned ones. The only way to guarantee a fresh oyster, it was decided, was to serve it attached to its shell — a guarantee of freshness still practiced in France today.

A man shucks oysters at a Paris market

I've had a few customers from Europe who have voiced their "disappointment" that the oysters were not left attached to the bottom shell. For them, part of the pleasure of enjoying oysters is the final freeing of the meat from the shell — that "proof of freshness" I mentioned earlier. I explain that this style of shucking is purely a North American thing, and suggest that the next time they go in search of oysters, they ask the shucker to leave the meat attached to the shell. I'm certainly happy to oblige them.

KEEP YOUR EYE ON THE OYSTER

Even if you're an expert shucker, it's inevitable that you'll cut yourself at one time or another. How badly depends on how much attention you pay to the oyster. I make it a rule to keep my eye on the oyster at all times. If you look away while shucking, you may find a knife tip in your hand. You may also get cut by the shell, which can be razor-sharp.

When you do get cut, use common sense. Wash the cut with soap and water; apply a little antibacterial cream and cover the cut with a bandage. If it's a deep cut, you may want to see a doctor. If you must keep working, as I've had to do on rare occasions, super glue will work in a pinch, with surgical gloves over top. But I normally recommend calling it quits for the day.

Shucker Paddy at work

PRESENTATION

Oysters should please the eye and the taste buds. You want them to look as if Mother Nature opened them herself. That means free of cuts, grit, and bits of shell. As you're shucking, keep an eye, too, on the hinge area. The shell just under the cartilage can break away and become annoying. Folds in the hinge can also collect a lot of silt, so be aware of this and keep the oyster clean.

There are lots of creatures in the ocean, and a few of them love oysters. I've found worms, fish, crabs, krill, sponge, barnacles, mussels, and even tiny sea urchins both on the outside and venturing inside. This is natural, so don't be alarmed. Calcium-boring worms don't enter the oyster, as that would kill the host. Instead, they live within the folds and feast on the calcium in the shell. Once the oyster hits fresh water, as in a tray of ice, any worms present will get out of there fast. If a worm appears while you're shucking, it's easy to remove.

Once oysters are shucked, they must be served immediately.

Platter: I normally use an aluminum pie plate. They're inexpensive, durable, and dishwasher-safe. To prevent slipping, place a paper napkin and three oyster shells under the ice. For larger gatherings, I suggest a stainless-steel tray.

Ice: Oysters prefer crushed ice, and there are several crushers on the market. Shovel the ice into the pie plate or tray and level it gently with your hand so the oysters can nestle into it.

Oysters: A full tray of opened oysters shows best, so fill it up! The hinges should point to the middle of the tray and the cup should reach the rim. This way, you can layer and stack the oyster shells without touching the meat.

Shells: I use the top shells to separate different varieties of oysters on one tray. This technique also helps to fill up the tray. Sometimes I put down a lot of shells for just one oyster.

Horseradish: Before grating, I peel the fresh root and soak it in water for three to five days. This intensifies the flavor and gives it a clean, steely finish. We always grate horseradish to order so it won't turn grey or dry up. I cut the soaked root into pieces 5 inches (12.5 cm) long and grate it lengthwise. The strands come out long and thin, and accentuate the flavor of the root.

Seaweed: I love this wavy green plant with its fresh ocean scent. When boiled, it turns a lovely blue-green. We often get rockweed, which grows on rocks close to shore. I'll only use it, however, when it comes packed around a shipment of oysters. I don't like the idea of pulling it from the sea for a one-time garnish. If you dry rockweed, you can manipulate it into fantastic shapes for your plate.

Lemons: Some customers get upset if there are no lemons to be had. To prepare, cut off both ends, then turn the lemon on its end and make four equal cuts to produce eight wedges. If the lemons are extra-fat, cut them in half first then into 16 wedges. Since pre-cut wedges can get slimy by the end of the day, I always cut lemons to order.

THE BAD OYSTER

When I'm shucking at the bar, I keep a pint glass handy and put all of my B-string oysters into it. These are the oysters that are not pretty enough for the half-shell — the meat is cut, the shell is broken or is otherwise unpresentable to my eye — but still perfectly good for chowder or other oyster dishes.

However, when an oyster is old, dry, and unhappy, you'll know it. Sour, pungent smells of sulfur and fermented leaves tell you right away to throw it out.

The more oysters you shuck, the greater your chances of coming across a bad one. A bad oyster is one that died in the shell but retained its seal and looks and feels good, right up to the moment it's opened. This is especially true in spring. If a North Eastern oyster happens to get caught in ice, it will freeze in its shell and die. The same fate will befall an oyster silted over in a storm; it will perish from lack of oxygen.

Come spring thaw, some of these oysters may be harvested and sold to consumers unwittingly. You'll be enjoying the winter plumpness of the oyster, its salty sweetness, the beautiful ease of shucking for busy crowds, and then it happens: you crack the hinge and the smell envelops you. It's amazing how fast and how far it will travel. Suddenly people 50 feet away are wondering what's going on. You can almost see the smell — thick, deep, sulfurous. It's the smell of oceany death.

When this happens, be prepared. Have a small bucket of water near your shucking station at all times and place the offending oyster, shell and all, in the water right away, then clean your shucking area.

Next step, burn some butcher's twine if you have any. It's not as over-powering as incense, but just as effective. At Ceílí we have turf — true Connemara turf, the true scent of the west of Ireland. A quick burn of the turf, and all is well again.

A Sneaky Oyster, as the name implies, will evade even the best shucker. It looks good and smells fine, yet when you bite into it you get a funky, musty bitterness in the finish. If you cover your oysters with sauce or just shoot them back, you won't even notice it. Your only defence against a Sneaky is to keep a close eye on the oyster meat as you shuck. If it's a little off-color, gray in the gills, or bruised-looking, your oyster is probably off. Smell it to be sure or simply discard it.

Another baddie is the Battleship Gray, with its smooth, gray body and black fleshy folds. Then there's The Jumper, an oyster that has deterio-rated so much that it is loose in the shell and almost jumps across the counter when shucked. The Black Meanie, meanwhile, actually turns black and has the most offensive smell, while an Ol' Smoky looks and wafts like smoke but may not smell that strong. Also beware of The Liquidator, an oyster transformed into a blackish-gray puddle. It may or may not be smelly.

While an oyster may smell, it won't necessarily harm you. A truly harmful oyster won't have a foul smell or an unhealthy look or taste. It may come from areas affected by a toxic algae and be deemed unfit for human consumption. Under government-run Fisheries and Oceans regulations, these oysters can't be harvested. As long as you buy your oysters from a reputable purveyor, with the harvest tags intact, you should be safe.

CHAPTER FOUR

THE PLEASURE OF OYSTERS: RECIPES

Oysters are to the French what pasta is to the Italians or what coffee is to North Americans which says a lot about our respective cultures, but let's leave that discussion for another book! Blessed with more than 2,000 miles (3200 km) of coastline, France boasts some of the finest oyster beds in the world, a claim that dates back to Roman times. Its 3,400 oyster growers produce more oysters than any other country in the world — approximately 130,000 tons annually — and 90 percent of those oysters are consumed by the French themselves. No wonder oysters abound in the social, cultural and culinary life of France.

In the nineteenth century there were three oyster capitals in the world: Paris, London, and New York. Although great oysters — and many of them — are served in New York and London, Paris continues to be regarded by many as the world's capital for oysters.

To this day, the city offers countless opportunities to socialize over oysters, including the classics from Cancale, Marennes Oléron and Arcachon. The coast of France also offers fantastic oyster discoveries.

A Frenchman in Marennes enjoys a plateful of local oysters

119

Virtually anywhere along the country's coastline, including the Mediterranean, delicious oysters can be found. Usually a particular local wine is recommended by the host in order to properly optimize both the taste of the oyster and the merroir experience overall. Much like French wine-growing regions, France's oyster-cultivation areas are often informally referred to by the term "cru." One of the best things about enjoying oysters along the French coast, though, is the price — about half of what you would pay in Paris!

The ubiquitous oyster is available every day for the enjoyment of the citizens of France — in oyster bars, in restaurants specializing in seafood, at little market stalls or kiosks on street corners, from vendors at the seaside, in baskets or boxes overflowing with freshly caught bivalves in growers' sheds... But the ringing in of the Christmas season catapults France's love affair with the oyster to dizzying new heights.

In the week between Christmas Eve and New Year's Day, 50 percent (yes, *50* percent) of the country's annual oyster production is consumed. That's a lot of oysters by anyone's count. I recently came across an article that appeared several years ago in *The Observer*.

Left: Christmastime along the Champs-Elysées in Paris
Right: Villagers gather oyesters along the beach in Cancale, circa 1900

In it, author and confirmed oyster addict Lisa Hilton describes the festive scene in Paris: "At Christmas on the Ile St-Louis, my neighbors wished each other *Joyeux Noël* in the streets, with balsa-wood boxes packed with ice and seaweed dangling from their arms, the oyster as essential an ingredient of the Christmas feast as the Brussels sprout in Blighty. The Parisian oyster has retained its democratic ubiquity. From the street markets of the Rue Mouffetard and Rue de Buci to the dark, serious brasseries surrounding the Bourse, they are everywhere."

While most of us may not have a chance to enjoy the salty, sensuous pleasure of oysters at a Christmas *Reveillon* in Paris any time soon, let's take a cue from the oyster-loving French and consider a little entertaining with oysters ourselves.

PLANNING AN OYSTER PARTY

So you'd like to have an oyster party. What a great idea! First, however, make sure you're inviting people who love oysters. You'd be surprised how often I end up sitting, rather than shucking, at a big party because nobody wants to eat raw oysters! Once you've established your guest list, you'll need an oyster menu. Depending on the size of the party, you can serve a full tasting of varietals or simply order lots of a single variety.

Small: A party of four to 20 people can be just as much fun as a large one, and easier to control. Ask your local oyster bar if you can order takeout, then set up a tasting. Start with an Atlantic oyster; then add a Pacific and a Kumamoto, if possible. If you can afford to splurge, buy all five species. To make the party stress-free, have your oyster provider or fishmonger open the oysters for you and put the caps back on. When it's time to serve, simply lift off the cap and *voilà!* If you prefer to shuck the oysters yourself, do it in the kitchen, where the guests will end up anyway. (See Oyster Shucking Techniques, Chapter 3.)

Medium: For Christmas, other special occasions or just because everyone's in the mood, 20 to 50 people can go through a lot of oysters. In fact, for this size of gathering, you may want to hire a professional shucker. I suggest serving one, two or three varieties maximum, mostly Atlantic. If you have the space, set up a separate worktable opposite the bar to give the event some flow and to encourage mingling. Spread out the food so people don't crowd one area. If you're a good shucker, you can probably handle a medium-size party, but you'll definitely need to enlist friends to play host and tend bar.

Large: For parties of 50 and more, it's time to call in the experts. At three oysters per person — a conservative estimate — you'll need 150 oysters minimum and will most likely cut yourself trying to keep up!

Celebrating a bounty of Marennes – Oléron oysters in France

BRINGING HOME THE BIVALVES

Be sure to give your fishmonger at least a week's notice so he or she can order what you need, either whole or shucked. Oysters in the shell are pretty hardy, so you don't have to be extra-careful about bringing them home. If you're buying a lot, however, ask the fish market for a Styrofoam container left over from a lobster shipment. Fill it with oysters, then ice. If you're traveling a great distance in warm weather, drain the melted ice every six to ten hours so the creatures don't sit in freshwater. Top with fresh ice and keep going. If you're not traveling far, or just have a few oysters, double-bag the bivalves and top with a bag of ice (or frozen peas) to keep them cold.

If you plan to serve oysters often, I would invest in a Coleman cooler, lined with plastic for easy cleaning. Just rinse the oysters, place them in the cooler and top with ice.

WORKSPACE

Place your oyster bar in a central location or opposite the bar. Too many times I have been relegated to a far corner and shucked only half the oysters I brought while guests wondered where the oysters were. I suggest that you have the caterer and the shucker decide on the best location to make the most of the experience for your guests.

If you are shucking in the kitchen, protect your countertops by placing a damp cloth under the shucking board and trays. A damp cloth also keeps the board from slipping. A drop cloth on the floor is another good idea, especially if carpets are involved.

A lovely rich Malpeque

When working with oysters, nothing beats the great outdoors. The shells can go anywhere, the liquor on your toes or in the grass, and all that fresh air makes you hungry for more. And it doesn't matter if you're holding a casual get-together or shucking for a formal wedding.

OYSTER TUNES

Set your party apart with some great music. I had a chat with the oysters recently and they confided that they were happiest with a little East Coast fiddle music, a bit of Cajun, or some funky R&B. Of course, some N'awlins jazz and blues always fits the bill.

THE DRINKS LIST

Ask your local caterer or wine/beer supplier for suggestions.

When customers at The Ceílí Cottage ask what to drink with oysters, my usual answer is "whatever makes you happy." And there is certainly some truth to that statement (Guinness and Irish Flats aside!). We once had a group of sommeliers bring in several thousand dollars' worth of wine and Champagne, and I prepared a variety of oysters to see if we could make a definitive match. After a few hours of rigorous, grueling, nose-to-the-grindstone work, the sommeliers came to the same conclusion: There is no one, perfect match for oysters. There are many.

I can, however, offer a few suggestions. Lighter drinks, such as beer and wine, tend to enhance the taste of oysters. Although many guests insist on starting their evening with a martini, I find harder liquors tend to overpower the oyster's flavor. Here are a few of my favorite drinks, with oysters to match.

Champagne

The drink of royalty has long accompanied oysters. I find that dry bruts and blanc de blancs pair beautifully with oysters. Of course, the best oysters to enjoy with Champagne are Spéciales and Fines de Claires from France, with their elegant flavors of sea salt and crisp melon. The metallic taste of the Belon oyster is also enhanced by Champagne's tiny bubbles. Definitely worth a try!

White Wine

When Champagne doesn't suit your mood or pocketbook, most oysters will pair wonderfully with a clean, crisp, dry, white wine with citrus and mineral notes. My favorites include Muscadet, Sancerre, unoaked Chardonnay, Chablis, Sauvignon Blanc, Pinot Grigio or a dry Riesling. Stay away from sweeter whites and buttery, oaky varieties.

Martin Malivoire, a small Canadian winemaker, ordered some Muscat cuttings from France for his Niagara vineyard. He received the cuttings as ordered, grafted them and tended the vines for a few years until the first fruit appeared. Much to his surprise, the grapes were not Muscat, but Melon — an old Burgundian variety used to produce Muscadet, a classic oyster wine. Fortunately, Martin loves oysters, so he decided to produce Martin's Oyster Wine (labeled Melon) some 1,550 miles (2,500 km) from the ocean in Niagara Ontario in limited edition.

Red Wine

Yes, red wine does go with oysters, if that's what you like to drink. For best results, choose lighter grapes such as Pinot Noir and Gamay and shy away from big, full-bodied wines — although I do know some oyster lovers who swear by a big Shiraz with creamier oysters such as the *C. gigas*.

Beer

Different beers work with different oysters. One famous combo is Guinness stout with oysters. Trouble is, the oysters referred to are Wild Irish Flats, or *O. edulis*, some of the best of which are cultivated by the Kellys of Kilcolgan, Ireland. This big, meaty, briny creature with the dry metallic finish practically cries out for Guinness's dry-roasted malts, especially when it's the

unpasteurized Irish variety. The result is a match made in, well, Ireland. The best place by far to savor this experience is seated by the kitchen window at Moran's Oyster Cottage, outside Galway. (See page 205.)

I think the Belgians got it right by brewing a different beer for every day of the year. Their "spontaneous fermentation" process lets Mother Nature guide the beer, much as she helps out with the oysters. Like wine and oysters, lighter, drier beers work best. White beers and lighter golden ales, with their soft, moussy texture, are excellent with oysters. Liefman's Goudenband is a rare find, but well worth searching out. Light American lagers and Japan's Sapporo beer also complement oysters.

Patrick's Oyster Stout

Oyster stout is a beer that stems from the United Kingdom. London dockworkers in the 1800s ground up oyster shells and used them as finings to clarify the beer. Popular belief was that oysters were good for you, and stout was good for you, so why not make a healthy cocktail of the two?

The Biddy Early in Ireland was said to be a local "healer" with a magical elixir that would cure all from lame horses to pneumonia. One hundred years later, a cobalt blue bottle found behind the house where she was known to practice revealed a residue of oysters and stout beer, and thus the Biddy Early Brewery resurrected this namesake beer in the late 1990s and continues to brew today.

I first started brewing an oyster stout in 1996. Now I work with a local brewer in Ontario — Barley Days Brewery — and use 1000 Green Gables oysters from P.E.I. in every batch we make. Shell and all is tossed into the kettle to marry all of the flavors of the oyster — liquor, meats, and earthy mineral shell. The result, some say, is magical and may cause friskiness.

Spirits

I am usually too busy to mix drinks and shuck oysters at the same time, so I ignored spirits until fairly recently. With the wave of interest in flavored vodkas and other concoctions, I found I had created two signature toppings that worked well in making dirty martinis. See Signature Toppings for my take on how to mix a dirty martini.

Pimm's Paddy No. 39 Champion Cup

Pimm's in the summer on the patio with a plate of oysters in the sunshine — or at Wimbledon, watching tennis: what could be finer? Pimm's was created in the 1820s by James Pimm, who opened his first oyster bar in the City of London around 1823. To this day there is a Pimm's Oyster House at Coogee Rooftop in Coogee, by the beach, in New South Wales, Australia. Bottoms up, down under!

Pimm's No. 1 Cup 1¾ oz (50 mL)
Gin 1 oz (28 mL)
ShuckerPunch lemonade 100ml 3.5oz (100 mL)
Ginger ale 1¾ oz (50 mL)
Lemon, lime slices 1¾ oz (50 mL)
Cucumber
G & C (gin and cucumber) matchsticks (see page 149)
Mint sprig
Ice

Makes one 8 oz (228 mL) cocktail

(Recipe continued)

Pimm's Paddy No. 39 Champion Cup *(Continued)*

In a bartender's shaker:

Fill ¾ with ice cubes

Add Pimms No. 1 Cup, ShuckerPunch Lemonade (see page 131), ginger ale, squeeze 1 wedge of lemon, and lime, and 1 slice of cucumber.

Stir the cocktail so as not to bruise.

Fill a glass with ice cubes.

Strain the Pimm's into the fresh glass.

Garnish with lemon, lime, cucumber and the G & C matchsticks

Toss in a smart sprig of mint.

Serve — often

Oysters pairing: English Natives, whether Pinney's of Orford, Richard Haward's of West Mersea, Colchester, or Carlingford rock oysters from Carlingford Lough, Ireland.

If you can be at Wimbledon to sip this cocktail — all the better!

Ceílí Cottage Caesar
(originating from Starfish Oyster Bed and Grill circa 2002)

For a mini version, serve this as a shooter.

Rim a 16-oz (500 mL) glass with a wedge of lime, then dip the glass in dried, crushed dulse seaweed.

Fill glass with ice, and squeeze in the juice of a lime.

Add 1 oz (30 mL) of premium vodka or vodka infused with fresh horseradish (See Vodka Root on page 148)

Add 2 to 3 shakes of Tabasco and Worcestershire sauce, a pinch of fresh grated horse-radish, and a pinch of dried dulse. Top with Clamato juice.

Add a skewered shucked oyster (or clam), with its liquor, for extra goodness.

All hail the Céílí Caesar!
One for you, Brutus?

Oyster Shooters

I am more of a sipper than a shooter type of guy, but it is fun to come up with new and different drinks for guests on request. While traditional shooters involve vodka, we've concocted a variety that match and include the oyster as a main ingredient.

Vodka Shooter: There are many variations on this one, so have fun. Use a firm, plump East Coast oyster big enough to fill half the glass. Top with chilled vodka and go! For a twist, add fresh lemon and/or lime juice, hot sauce, and some of our Horseradish Vodka

Gin Shooter: I'd pair gin with the *C. gigas* Pacific oyster, which is small enough to fit in the glass. Just fill and serve. For a twist, add a little lemon or lime juice, our Cucumber Gin and a splash of tonic water.

Shooter Royale: One day I came up with this multi-layered drink. Take a few of your favorite oysters of different sizes, layer them in a tall glass with vodka, and top with a little cocktail sauce and lemon and lime juice.

Beer Shooter: The boys at Shaw's of Chicago tell me that the oyster-and-beer shooter was invented in San Francisco in the gold-rush days to satisfy prospectors looking to spend their money.

The Shuck and Tipple — oyster & whiskey pairings

Michael Jackson — the Beer Hunter, not the singer/songwriter — once suggested to me that I try Oban whiskey and oysters. While traveling in Skye, I came across the Talisker Distillery and the Isle of Skye Oyster Farm not 150 feet (45 meters) away from the distillery. It dawned on me that the oysters and the whiskey share the same environment of salt, fresh water, ocean air, seaweed and wood. A couple of years later, I happened to land Irish, Scottish, English, and French oysters at The Ceílí Cottage, and I just so happened to have matching regional whiskies for each of the oyster varietals. So I began to experiment with how to match oysters and whiskey. After long deliberations, I figured it out, and I invite you to try this simple but effective technique: the Shuck & Tipple.

1. Shuck the oyster, cup down, to hold the liquor.

2. Slide the oyster into your mouth, but leave a tidbit of oyster liquor in the shell.

3. Take a two-bite chew, aerate, and think about the flavors developing on your palate.

4. Pour the designated whiskey into the freshly emptied shell.

5. Sip the whiskey from the shell. The whiskey will marry with the oyster liquor and flavor the dram with sea salt, earthy notes, and wet stone. I highly recommend trying this method — especially while in Scotland in Stranraer for their oyster festival.

WHISKIES THAT MATCH

If you can find whiskey in close proximity to where the oyster was raised, that would be the best selection. Whiskies that work well include:

Powers — Ireland
Forty Creek Confederation Oak Cask — Canada
Elijah Craig — United States
Rock Oyster — Scotland (blended from ocean-kissed
    casks; salty and smoky; great with oysters)

ShuckerPunch — electrolyte replacement & cocktail base
Makes 1 cocktail

3 oz (90 mlL) oyster liquor
½ oz (15 mL) simple syrup (recipe page 138)
Juice from 1 lemon
½ teaspoon dulse seaweed powder
Enough ice to fill shaker

Place all ingredients into a bartender's shaker, cover with the lid, and shake.

Pour into a glass filled with ice and serve.

To make it into a cocktail add 1 to 2 oz (30 to 60 ml) vodka or gin of your choice.

Simple Syrup

1 cup (250 mL) water
1 cup (250 mL) white sugar

In a small saucepan bring the water to a boil. Add sugar, reduce heat, and simmer mixture, stirring continuously, until the sugar has dissolved. Let cool completely before using in a drink mix. You can make as much or as little of this as you need (a double batch is usually enough for a party). It'll keep in a glass jar in the fridge, for up to 1 month.

OCEAN SMOOTHIE

In a blender, combine two oysters and one batch of ShuckerPunch (page 137) and blend until smooth. Remember: *C. gigas* oysters = more ocean flavor.

The Kelpie, A Green Ocean Smoothie

Blending kelp, cucumber and lemon with cayenne creates an invigorating boost. The oyster only accentuates this — increasing protein, omega 3s, zinc, selenium, associated minerals and micro algae! The goodness and savor of the sea, in a glass…

1 Empire apple whole, stem removed
½ English cucumber
1 cup (or 250 mL) or 2-3 kelp fresh leaves

If your kelp leaves are dried – that is, salt free – then soak them over-night, in 1 cup (250 mL) of water. You can use other dried seaweeds – Japanese wakame; or laver, whether from Wales or from Kobe, Japan – also soaked overnight.

Juice of 1 lemon
¼ (125 mL) cup fresh cilantro
¼ (1 mL) teaspoon cayenne pepper
2 whole *C. gigas* oysters — and their liquor
pinch of powdered dulse seaweed for the top

Place all the ingredients, including oyster liquor, and soaked water from the kelp into blender and blend until smooth. Add a pinch of dulse powder across the top for color and taste.

WHAT TO DO WITH THE SHELLS?

The only problem with holding an oyster party is that you are left holding the bag — and it's heavy. In fact, oyster shells are about the heaviest garbage you'll ever come across. Fortunately, they're completely organic and can be placed in your municipal organics bin.

If you've hired a caterer, the staff will take the shells away along with the rented glasses. If you're on your own, however, I suggest double-bagging your garbage can and changing the bag when it's just half-full so it's easier to move.

During the party, keep the garbage can out of sight behind the bar. When I'm shucking, I place an empty aluminum tray in front of the station where guests can pile their spent shells. When it's full, I just dump it into the bin when nobody's looking. Nice and neat. I only remove the bin after all the guests have left.

Some of my catering clients like to keep the shells and use them on their driveway or garden paths. The shells break down eventually and make a nice white pavement when bleached by the sun. If you don't want your garden to smell like a wharf, I'd suggest boiling the shells for a few minutes, or let the raccoons do the cleaning overnight.

Since Hurricane Sandy swept through New York in 2012, an oyster-reef restoration project has been running in Manhattan. The Billion Oyster Project (BOP), set up by the New York Harbor School, partners with participating restaurants to have shucked shells returned to the ocean. The BOP receives shells, processes them, and then uses them to create oyster reefs in the New York Harbor. The shell reefs attract spat oysters to set, mingle, and build a healthy ecosystem — a non-harvest zone — filtering the water, and doing their helpful oystery thing.

Oyster shells have an incredible number of other uses. The shells from my restaurant are recycled by an egg producer, who grinds them up and feeds them to their chickens. Since they're a natural form of calcium, the ground oyster shells help promote a hard eggshell. Ground oyster shell is also used in calcium pills and herbal remedies. Kids love the shells for arts and crafts — painted, the frilly *C. gigas* shell makes a very nice Santa Claus. The Olympia makes great earrings.

In winter, I like to use crushed oyster shell on the sidewalk in front of my restaurant instead of salt or sand. The shells contain naturally occurring salt and, when crushed, work like sand. There's no slipping and it's environmentally friendly.

One customer told me he places wet shells in the fireplace, a few at a time. As the shells heat up, they pop and crackle with different colors from the calcium and escaping gases.

Can you guess how many oysters follies stars
Lois and Ruth Waddell consumed?

RECIPES

One night when I was out catering, shucking on my own for 100 hungry people, a nice young fella asked me, "How do you like to eat your oysters?" "Just on their own," I replied, "in the natural oyster liquor, a taste of the ocean they came from. That taste," I continue, "cannot be duplicated. If sauce or lemon was meant to be put on top of oyster, then Mother Nature would have placed the sauce tree and a lemon tree next to the oyster bed. Besides, by the time you've topped your one oyster with sauce, I've knocked back three … naked. Is there any other way?"

Apparently there is. In the oyster world, there are hundreds if not thousands of different ways to top, poach, stew, grill, smoke, roast, fry, and toss oysters, from appetizers to desserts. I've put together a few of what I consider the most essential and enjoyable in my oyster bar world.

Most recipes think of the oyster as a "singular entity," just use whatever oyster you can find. But in my shuckin' around, I've found that some oysters are better for cooking than others. Certain meats hold up better to heat; others shrink away to nothing. Some add big flavors and textures; some are neutral, and can work with any sauce; and some just shouldn't be cooked at all.

BEST COOKING VARIETIES

For cooking or frying oysters it's best to use plump, large, meaty oysters.

Atlantic East Light in flavor, these work well with sauces and for cooking. They can be neutral to salty, so taste a few first and adjust your seasoning. Some Northern water P.E.I./N.B./N.S./Maine oysters will work, but only in season when they are fattest, enjoyed on the half-shell.

Connecticut to Florida, and along the gulf: Here you can find great, fat, meaty oysters, and at a fair price. When it comes to cooking oysters, it's best to look for the largest/best-priced oysters since you'll be spending additional money on other ingredients.

Pacific oysters These are great for cooking. They're fat, meaty, and plump for most of the year. They have a bigger flavor profile, so think of these oysters as an ingredient that will impart a great, oystery/seaweedy/earthy note to the finished dish. These *C. gigas* oysters are the number one oyster grown around the world, and at the fast rate they grow, they are often less expensive than local oysters. Again, look for the best price for more oysters in your dish!

Galway natives — *O. edulis* — with garlic, butter, and breadcrumbs cannot be beat. The texture is very toothsome and meaty, and the flavor combination is classic. A lot of ancient European recipes would use this oyster as a main ingredient, including the Original Oyster Stout of the early 1800s in London.

OYSTER ON THE OPEN SHELL

Any oyster is a delight eaten this way but some are worth a special mention:

Kumamoto: Due to the size and cost of these perfect oysters, they are best enjoyed on the half-shell, naked or with a drizzle of mignonette at the most.

Olympia: These are among the rarest commercially grown oysters in the world, native only to North America on the Pacific side and with only a handful of growers producing them. This makes the Olympia a taste experience to be sought out. A regular customer loved the Olympia and got giddy whenever the Olys landed. His regular order, when he could get them, was 48 Olympia, a bottle of Chablis, and, he said, "Don't talk to me." He loved them so much, he didn't want his enjoyment to be interrupted.

OYSTER LIQUOR

Oyster Liquor — is a real snapshot of the body of water the oyster came from. French oyster etiquette states that this liquor is just seawater, and to enjoy the oyster itself we must tip it into the tray of shells and let the oyster rest. The true liquor of the oyster will fill the shell from within the oyster itself — this is called the *véritable essence de l'huître.*

When shucking, seawater, or liquor, makes a wet mess if you do not contain and control your shucking station. A few years ago, I developed my shucking tray for just this reason, and started collecting oyster liquor. At first I kept a blended liquor, from west and east, north and south, oysters from away, all combined in my tray, which I then tipped into a container and stored in my freezer. I was saving it for my oyster stout experiments.

Then one day it came to me: oyster liquor is an ingredient. It's all of the flavors of the ocean and shoreline caught between two shells. How do chefs brine fish? They make a brine solution of salt and water, maybe adding some spices. What's the most natural brine you can find? Seawater. Where do you find seawater in Toronto, or any interior city? In oysters. If you shuck various different oysters and collect the liquor from all of them, you get a blend, like in whiskies. But what if you focus, and collect location-specific oyster liquors? You get a single bed oyster liquor — a merroir-specific ingredient used to subtly flavor foods. You can use it for anything that requires salt and water — a lobster boil, oyster stout, a Malpeque martini, fish batter, pie pastry, meat curing, salt water taffy.

HOW TO CAPTURE AND PROCESS OYSTER LIQUOR

Shuck in a pan. There, it's as simple as that. A square cookie sheet, a round pie pan, or if you want to be fancy, use the stainless-steel oyster tray and the all-Canadian Shuckin'Puck — it'll all work.

Shuck in a tray, capture the liquor, and once the tray is full, pour the liquor into a container (a Mason jar works well). Strain through a paper coffee filter or cheesecloth to avoid getting a lot of shell, grit, and silt in the liquor. You can freeze the liquor until you have amassed enough for your use (I recommend using a plastic container for the freezer). Label and date the container. Blend the liquors of many oysters or focus on a single bed oyster, it's up to you.

TOPPINGS, IF YOU MUST

Lemon slices, cut to order
Freshly grated horseradish

Peel and soak the horseradish, place in a container of water, cover, and let it soak in the fridge for several days before grating to bring out the flavor and heat of the root.

ON GRATING HORSERADISH

A lesson learned from an ol' coot, a customer from my Starfish days: Soak horseradish in water for a week (in the fridge). Cut the root into 3-inch (7.5 cm) pieces and grate with the grain (not against the grain) to get long, thin strands.

SHUCKER PADDY SIGNATURE TOPPINGS

Vodka Root

Running late for a wedding catering gig, I didn't have time to grate fresh horseradish on site. I knew the groom liked his vodka and horseradish, so I took a 4-cup (1 L) Mason jar, filled it to the brim with freshly grated horseradish, topped it off with vodka, secured the lid, and went on my merry way. When I arrived at the venue 30 minutes late and opened the jar, there was an explosion of boozy horseradish goodness: the vodka had activated the enzymes of the root. The root picked up vodka, the vodka picked up horseradish. It was perfection.

My Malpeque Martini

Note: The root stays wet and crisp; the vodka "pickles" the vegetable. Serve the vodka root as a garnish, direct from the Mason jar. Reserve the liquid and make a fantastic horseradish dirty martini or Paddy's Céilí Cottage Caesar.

1 horseradish root, freshly grated
Vodka, enough to immerse the root (about 2 cups)

Fill a 4-cup (1 L) Mason jar with freshly grated horseradish and cover with vodka. Seal jar and refrigerate for at least 30 minutes.

Paddy's G & C: Gin and Cucumber
Makes 4 cups (1 L)

The crisp cucumber goes well with firm, plump oysters. Gin Cuke can also be used to make a dirty gin martini, and in a Céilí Caesar, or even a perfectly refreshing Oyster Shooter.

1 English cucumber, skin on, cut into matchsticks
Gin

Fill a 4-cup (1 L) Mason jar with cucumber matchsticks and cover with gin. Chill in the fridge until ready to serve your oysters.

THE TREFOIL

These three sauces are most often most often served with oysters: cocktail, mignonette, and a hot sauce. Of course, you can buy all of these pre-made, with massively great flavors and tastes, but here are some that I'll make at the bar or for events.

Cocktail Sauce, American Style
Makes as much as you like

In the United States, oyster culture states that cocktail sauce is mixed by the customer, according to the ancient and secret recipe that grandpappy told them. On a tray of oysters, you'll find a ramekin of uncut straight-up ketchup and one with prepared horseradish. As grandpappy said, mix two spoonfuls of ketchup, with three-quarters of a spoon of horseradish, add 1 drop of Tabasco sauce, and mix.

Ketchup

Prepared horseradish
Tabasco sauce (optional)

In a jar, combine all three ingredients — in quantities that suit you —
seal, and shake well. Taste and adjust seasonings until it's a consistency
and flavor you like.

Tip - drain the horseradish in a colander or through cheesecloth
to remove as much liquid as possible — this keeps the cocktail sauce
thicker.

Deluxe Cocktail Sauce
Makes 4 cups (1 L)

1 shallot, minced
¼ cup (60 mL) gherkin pickles, minced
¼ cup (60 mL) capers, drained and minced
2 tbsp (30 mL) oyster liquor
2 tbsp (30 mL) fresh lemon juice
1 tsp (5 mL) freshly ground black pepper
2 cups (500 mL) high-quality ketchup
1 cup (250 mL) chili sauce
½ cup (125 mL) prepared horseradish, drained
1 tbsp (15 mL) Worcestershire sauce

Place the shallot, gherkins, capers, oyster liquor, lemon juice, and
black pepper into a food processor and process until fine. (You can
also finely mince all ingredients by hand.) Transfer the mixture to a

bowl, then add the ketchup, chili sauce, and drained horseradish and mix well. Add more lemon and pepper, to taste. Pour into a Mason jar and chill until shucking time.

ComeBack Sauce

So good, you'll come back for more.

Makes as much as you like

Cocktail sauce (fancy or regular)
Mayonnaise

In a bowl, whisk together equal parts cocktail sauce and mayonnaise.

Mignonette

Makes ½ cup (125 mL)

This is a simple, light vinaigrette. Mignonette was designed in France to cut the salinity, and minerality, of the native Belon/Flat oysters. You can create several delightful variations on this simple vinaigrette with seasonal tastes and flavors. For example, adding diced apple or pear, fresh basil or thyme.

3 shallots, finely minced
Freshly ground black pepper
½ cup (125 mL) vinegar

Place the minced shallots into a 4-cup (1 L) Mason jar. Season with black pepper. Pour in the vinegar. Seal with the lid and shake it up. That is all.

ShuckerPaddy's Hard Cider Mignonette
Makes 4 cups (1 L)

5 French shallots, finely minced
1 Granny Smith apple, unpeeled, finely minced
¼ tsp (1 mL) freshly ground black pepper, or more to taste
1 cup (250 mL or half a can) hard cider (Magner's from Ireland
    is a great one to use; go ahead and drink the other half)
2 cups (500 mL) apple cider vinegar

Place the minced shallots and apple into a 4-cup (1 L) Mason jar.
Season with black pepper. Pour in the hard cider (you may want to
take a sip, just to make sure it is good), and top off with the apple cider
vinegar. Seal with the lid and shake it up. Done.

Antoinette's Classic Champagne Mignonette
Makes about 3 cups (750 mL)

Apparently, there is such a thing as "leftover champagne" — although
I think if you have some, you might be doing it wrong. Fret not!
You can make Champagne Mignonette to adorn the royalty of
The Belon (*O. edulis*), Europe's native oyster!

6 French shallots, finely minced
Freshly ground black pepper
2 cups (500 mL) white wine vinegar
1 cup (250 mL) Champagne, flat or fresh, whatever you have
    lying around the château

Place the minced shallots into a 4-cup (1 L) Mason jar. Season with three turns of the pepper mill. Add the white wine vinegar, and then the Champagne vinegar. Whisper *Oh la la, c'est mignonette est magnifique!*

Mt. Fuji Mignonette
Makes about 3 cups (750 mL)

This mignonette is excellent for Kumamoto oysters *(C. sikaema).*

2 cups (500 mL) light rice wine vinegar
1 cup (250 mL) sake
4 spring onions, white and green parts, finely minced
2 sheets roasted nori seaweed (for sushi), cut into ¼ inch (5 mm)
    strips and finely julienned
⅛ tsp (0.5 mL) sesame oil (about 6 drops)

Place the onion and nori in a Mason jar. Add the rice wine vinegar, sake, and sesame oil. Seal the lid and shake well. Place the mignonette in the fridge to allow the seaweed to marry with the liquid for at least two hours. Drizzle a spoonful over a Kumo, and top the oyster with a few strands of dry nori.

The Emperor's New Mignonette
Serves you very well, indeed

This mignonette is best suited for Olympia oysters *(O. luridis)*.

0 white wine vinegar
0 fresh lemon juice
0 shallots, minced
0 freshly ground black pepper

Combine all of the ingredients in a Mason jar, seal the lid, shake it about, ladle 0 spoonfuls onto your Olympias. Then "sip your Chablis and don't talk to me."

Olympia oysters dressed with the Emperor's New Mignonette

HOT SAUCE

There are hundreds of different ways to make hot sauce, but none are quite like the first you've ever tried. I met Grace Noel in the kitchen at Rodney's Oyster House back in the 1990s. I quickly learned that Momma Grace came first, then the oyster, the crew, and the customer — in that order. If you adhered to this rule, the customer would be happy every time.

It's a lesson I learned and continue to remember: ingredients first, the people who prepare them, and then the customer. Grenada-born, Momma Grace had a knack for heat — flavorful heat, with just the right amount of kick. After staff meal one day — Momma Grace's sweat-inducing chicken with rice and peas, which could actually induce hiccups from the heat — I asked, "Hey, Momma Grace, when are you gonna give us the good stuff, the real heat, the stuff you cook at home?" She replied like always, with a little chuckle: "Ha ha. Oh no, son, you can't handle that, takes years of practice." I learned many things from Momma Grace: to use plastic wrap goggles when chopping peppers and onions, and how to pick and stew Scotch bonnet peppers to make a wicked hot sauce, with my added touch of ageing.

Grace's Barrel Aged XXX Peppa sauce

Wear surgical gloves when handling scotch bonnet peppers, please. Also, keep the oven vent on or make this outdoors, as the vinegar and bonnet vapor is very strong.

4 lb (2 kg) red, orange, and yellow scotch bonnet peppers (take out
    the green ones, you don't want them), stemmed and quartered
4 cups (1 L) apple cider vinegar
4 cups (1 L) white vinegar
½ cup (125 ml) wood chips (preferably from a whiskey barrel),
    as used for smoking

Place the peppers in a deep pot and add both vinegars. Bring to a boil. Reduce the heat, cover with the lid, and simmer for 1 hour, until the peppers are very soft. Remove the pot from the heat and let the stewed peppers cool to room temperature.

Once the stewed peppers are cool, use an immersion blender to purée until smooth (a food processor or blender will also work). Transfer the mixture to a Mason jar and refrigerate for a few days. The longer it ages, the deeper the flavor.

Fill a Mason jar with ½ cup (125 mL) of whiskey barrel chips. Pour the pepper sauce over top. Seal the jar. Set aside in a dark, cool place and let age for at least a week. (Place in your fridge if that's what you have available for cool and dark.) Shake the jar a few times during this process.

After a week or so, you'll notice a great "barrel age" finish. The longer the sauce sits, the better. (Tabasco sauce is barrel-aged for two years before commercial release.

OYSTERS À LA VIE EN ROSE

Sometimes, simple is better. Take 6 perfect East Coast oysters on the half-shell — Pemaquid or Glidden Point oysters from Maine — and lay them out. Sip the Champagne, then pour a little onto each oyster, watching the bubbles cascade over the brim of the oyster shell. Bring it up to your lips, and enjoy.

APPETIZERS

Liquored Fish

Organic Irish Salmon belly, sliced like sashimi
Clarenbridge Bay oyster liquor

Ready the fish by cutting a thin, oyster-shell-size slice of salmon belly; set it aside. Shuck the oyster, and place it "belly up" on the top shell, reserving the oyster liquor in the shell. Slip the salmon belly into the fresh brine, and allow it to "cure" while you bring it to the table.

Oyster Chowder
Serves 6

A "shellabratory" chowder to be enjoyed on fancy nights like New Year's Eve. This shows oysters to be enjoyed in three styles: a base, poached, and fried.

3 large potatoes, peeled and diced
2 tbsp + 1 tsp butter (35 mL)
6 stalks celery, finely chopped
4 shallots, minced
12 large oysters, shucked (such as Fanny Bay / *C. gigas),* shucked
5 cups (1.25 mL) whole milk
2 slices extra-thick, double-smoked bacon, cut into lardons
24 small oysters (such as Green Gables/Malpeques), shucked
12 panko-crusted oysters (BluePoint or Large Gulf/Chesapeake),
    for garnish

In a large saucepan on medium-high heat, boil potatoes in salted water until fork-tender, about five minutes. Drain well, then set aside.

In another large saucepan on low heat, melt 2 tbsp (30 mL) of the butter. Add the chopped celery and shallots, and sauté, without browning, until soft and shallots are translucent, about 10 minutes. Place the 12 large oysters on top of the celery mixture. Increase the heat to medium, cover, and cook (don't stir) for five minutes, or until the edges of the oysters ruffle like a tuxedo shirt. Using a slotted spoon, transfer the oysters to a bowl and set aside. Reduce the heat to medium-low.

Add the milk to the celery mixture and heat through, being careful not to boil. Return the cooked oysters to the saucepan and add 1 cup (250 mL) of the cooked potatoes. Using an immersion blender, purée the soup until smooth.

Line a plate with a paper bag or paper towel. Heat a heavy frying pan on medium heat. Add the bacon and fry until crisp, about five minutes. Using tongs, transfer the bacon to the plate to drain; reserve the pan. Fry your panko-crusted oyster in the bacon grease.

Melt the 1 tsp (5 mL) of butter in a large saucepan on medium-low heat. Add the 24 small oysters, cover, and cook until the oysters ruffle and are just cooked through, two to three minutes. Pour in the soup and the remaining potatoes and heat through, being careful not to boil the chowder.

To serve, divide the chowder among six warmed bowls, ensuring that the oysters are evenly distributed. Sprinkle each serving with bacon and garnish with two panko-crusted oysters, a wee dollop of unsalted butter, and a sprinkle of dulse seaweed powder.

MAINS

Steak & Oyster Pie with Oyster Stout Gravy

I suggest using Irish deep cupped oysters — Clarenbridge Bay, Harty's, Kelly's, Achill Island.

Use oyster liquor in the pastry instead of cold water and salt.

⅓ cup (75 mL) sunflower oil

2 lb (1 kg) stewing beef

3 tbsp (45 mL) all-purpose flour

Salt and freshly ground black pepper, to taste

2 tbsp (30 mL) unsalted butter

2 cups (500 mL) button mushrooms, quartered

2 Spanish onions, thinly sliced

½ tsp (2 mL) granulated sugar

1½ cups Guinness stout or Oyster Stout

1 cup (250 mL) beef broth

3 sprigs of fresh thyme

2 bay leaves

2 tbsp (30 mL) Worcestershire sauce

12 Pacific oysters or large, plump Atlantic oysters, shucked; oyster liquor reserved

1 lb (500 g) pie pastry (enough to line and top 4 to 6 ramekins)

Salt and freshly ground black pepper, to taste

1 egg, beaten, for egg wash

In a large Dutch oven over medium-high heat, heat 2 tbsp (30 mL) of the oil.

In a bowl, toss stewing beef in salt-and-pepper seasoned flour. Transfer to the pan and sear in the hot oil, stirring occasionally to ensure browning on all sides. Transfer the browned beef to a plate (reserve pan) and set beef aside.

To the reserved pan, melt 1 tbsp (15 mL) of the butter. Add the mushrooms and cook, stirring often, until browned. Transfer to the plate.

Add the remaining 1 tbsp (15 mL) of the butter. Add the onions and cook, stirring often, until softened and translucent. Add the sugar and continue cooking, stirring occasionally, until the onions have caramelized. Stir in the beer and beef stock, and bring to a boil.

Add in the browned beef and mushrooms, thyme, and bay leaves. Reduce the heat, cover with the lid, and simmer for 1½ hours.

Meanwhile, roll the pastry out to ¼-inch thick. Using a knife, cut out 6 rounds. Line 6 ramekins with pastry, cutting off any excess. Cover with a kitchen towel and set aside.

Using a slotted spoon, transfer the meat, mushrooms, and onions to a bowl and set aside. Cook the remaining sauce until thickened (this will be your gravy).

Meanwhile, shuck the 12 oysters, and divide them evenly among the ramekins. Top with equal portions of the reserved beef, mushrooms, and onions. Drizzle with oyster liquor. Top up each with the gravy. Cover with pie pastry, pinching the edges to seal. Using a paring knife, cut a small vent hole in the center of each pie. Brush the tops with the well-beaten egg wash.

Bake in a 400°F (200°C) oven for 30 to 35 minutes, until the gravy is bubbling and the pastry is golden.

Pastry

4 cups (1 L) all-purpose flour
1½ tsp (7 mL) salt (see Tip)
½ cup (125 mL) unsalted butter
½ cup (125 mL) lard or shortening
½ cup (125 mL) cool water (see Tip)
2 eggs

In a large mixing bowl, combine the flour and, if you are not using oyster liquor in the next step, salt. Add the butter and lard. Using electric beaters on medium-low speed, mix until the butter and lard is fully incorporated into the flour (it will have a sandy texture).

In a separate bowl, whisk together the water (or oyster liquor, if using) and eggs. Add all at once to the flour mixture. Mix just until the dough comes together.

Cover with plastic wrap and place the dough in the fridge to rest for 1 hour.

After chilling, the dough is ready to be used.

Tip - You can replace the salt and cool water with ½ cup (125 mL) strained oyster liquor.

Variations

For a simple pie when you don't want to fuss with pastry, use store-bought puff pastry on top and don't line the ramekins at all.

Shepherd's Pie In a saucepan of water, boil three stalks of salsify (oyster plant) and three to four potatoes until tender. Mash until smooth. Fill the ramekins with the steak and oyster filling, and top with the mash. Broil in oven until the mash reveals golden peaks.

Carpet Bagger Steak Frîtes with Casino Compound Butter
Serves 4

This is a classic from Australia in the 1950s, so why not use Sydney rock oysters, or Coffin Bay. Or use small Pacifics if you cannot get Australian oysters.

3 to 4 freshly shucked oysters per steak, depending on size of steak;
    liquor reserved
¼ cup (60 mL) Worcestershire sauce
2 tbsp (30 mL) fresh lemon juice
4 New York strip steaks (1 inch or thicker cut)
Salt and pepper, to taste
3 tbsp (45 mL) oil
1 cup (250 mL) beef broth
¼ cup (60 mL) butter, at room temperature

Place the shucked oysters in a glass bowl with all of the oyster liquor. Add the Worcestershire and the lemon juice, and let the oysters marinate for 30 minutes.

Using a sharp knife, cut a pocket into the side of each steak, big enough to stuff in three to four oysters. Put the oysters into each steak, fill the pockets with some of the marinade, and close with a toothpick. Season the steaks with salt and pepper. Let rest at room temperature for 30 minutes.

Heat the oil in a skillet over medium-high heat until it just starts to smoke. Sear the steaks for about 3 minutes per side for medium-rare (longer if you want them well done).

Transfer the cooked steaks to a warmed plate to rest; reserve pan.

To the reserved pan, add the beef stock and any remaining marinade, along with the butter, and cook over medium heat, stirring up any brown bits at the bottom of the pan, until the mixture is reduced slightly. Drizzle over the steak. Serve with a large pat of Casino Compound Butter on top and crispy frites.

Casino Compound Butter

Compound butter is a simple blend of softened butter and seasonings that are compressed into a log shape and chilled until set. "Pats" can then be cut off and used to flavor meat, fish, vegetables or, in our case, freshly shucked oysters. At Céilí Cottage we use this compound butter to prepare Toasted Oysters using a toaster oven on the bar, to tease and coerce customers into ordering several dozen at a time. (This butter would be equally at home on a perfectly grilled steak or grilled fish, just sayin'.)

I always make 2 cups (500 mL) of compound butter at a time, and then divide it into manageable portions and freeze.

TOASTED OYSTER

You'll need a pat of compound butter per oyster. Warm up your toaster oven to 450ºF (230ºC).

Shuck the oysters in a bowl, reserving the liquor. Take the oysters out of their shells, and let dry on a towel. Place the empty shells in the toaster oven and heat through. Once the shells are warmed, place the dried oysters back into each shell and top with a pat of compound butter. Broil in the toaster oven for four to five minutes, or until the tops are golden and bubbling. Get ready to make more...

Moran's Garlic Compound Butter
Makes 2 cups (500 mL)

2 cups (500mL) plus 1 tbsp (15mL) unsalted butter,
    at room temperature
6 cloves garlic, minced
2 cups (500 mL) plain breadcrumbs or panko

In a frying pan over medium heat, melt 1 tbsp (15 mL) of the butter. Add the garlic and sauté until softened and lightly caramelized. Set aside.

In a bowl, combine 2 cups (500 mL) of the butter and the sautéed garlic; mix thoroughly. Add the breadcrumbs and stir until well incorporated.

Divide the mixture into four equal portions. Form each portion into a log and place each onto a large square of plastic wrap. Cover tightly, twisting the ends to seal, and refrigerate or freeze until hardened. (If you freeze, thaw out a little before slicing or the butter might shatter instead of slicing into nice coins.)

Oysters Casino

2 tbsp (30 mL) olive oil
1 shallot, minced
2 garlic cloves, minced
2 cups (500 mL) butter, at room temperature
2 cups plain panko breadcrumbs
2 roma tomatoes, seeded and cut into small dice
1 roasted red pepper, seeded and cut into small dice
4 fresh basil leaves, finely chopped
6 slices of double-smoked bacon, fried until crispy and crumbled
Freshly ground black pepper

Oyster Stuffing

This stuffing is perfect to accompany a Thanksgiving feast or as a dish on its own with a side salad and an oyster stout. Make sure your bread is day-old. You can always dry fresh bread by arranging it on a large sheet pan and then baking it in a 250ºF (120ºC) oven for about 15 minutes; let cool completely before using.

16 slices bacon
6 tbsp (90 mL) unsalted butter, melted, plus more for greasing
    the pan
6 shallots, thinly sliced
4 stalks of celery, thinly sliced
40 medium New England oysters (Bluepoints or Pemaquid)
    shucked; liquor reserved
1 cup (500 mL) chicken broth
¼ cup (60 mL) bourbon (Woodford reserve), flamed to reduce
    the alcohol
⅓ cup (75 ml) chopped fresh flat-leaf parsley leaves
2 tbsp (30 mL) chopped fresh rosemary
2 tbsp (30 mL) chopped fresh thyme leaves
2 tbsp (30 mL) chopped fresh sage leaves
¼ tsp (1 mL) freshly grated nutmeg
⅛ tsp (0.5 mL) ground cloves
Salt and freshly ground black pepper, to taste
12 cups crusty bread (French, sourdough, cornbread or a
    combination, day-old is best)

In a large skillet over medium-high heat, cook bacon, stirring frequently, until crisp, about 10 minutes. Add ¼ cup (60 mL) of the butter and heat until melted. Add the shallots and celery, reduce the heat to medium, and cook, stirring occasionally, until vegetables are soft and translucent, about 10 minutes. Add oyster liquor, broth, bourbon, parsley, rosemary, thyme, sage, nutmeg, cloves, and salt and pepper. Increase heat to high, and bring to a boil; cook, stirring occasionally, for five minutes. Pour this mixture into a large bowl (remember to scrape the pan for the good bits!). Stir in the bread cubes and oysters. Set aside for 15 minutes to allow the flavors to marry.

Preheat the oven to 400°F (200°C). Spread the mixture evenly in a buttered 10-cup (2.5 L) baking dish and cover with foil. Bake for 30 minutes. Remove foil, drizzle with remaining ¼ cup (60 mL) melted butter over the top, and continue baking until the top is golden brown and crusty, about 15 minutes more. Serve immediately.

Pan Fried — Panko crusted Oysters

Crispy on the outside, soft and meaty on the inside, there's something summery about a great fried oyster. I prefer to pan-fry them, as you can keep a better eye on the oyster, browning it perfectly to your liking. A cast-iron pan works best. I use butter or bacon drippings to make the most decadent of pan-frys. Find the plumpest, meatiest oyster you can. Bluepoint and South are great on the East Coast of North America, and any beach-finished oyster from the West. The bigger the better. Shucked/gallon oysters work very well, and there's no shucking to do!

These are perfect served on the half-shell and in a Po' Boy Sandwich.

12 freshly shucked oysters; liquor reserved
1 cup (250 mL) seasoned flour (1 cup (250 mL) flour,
    ¼ tsp (1 mL) salt, and ¼ tsp (1 mL) black pepper)
1 egg, whisked
1 cup (250 mL) plain panko breadcrumbs
¼ cup (60 mL) butter
Bacon drippings (optional)
Paper bag (or paper towel if you don't have a paper bag to use)
Come Back Sauce, optional

Dry your oysters on a paper towel, and dry the shells as well. Spread the empty shells over a baking sheet and place in a 150°F (70°C) oven to warm up and dry off.

Meanwhile, set up a breading station: place the seasoned flour, egg wash, and panko in three separate bowls. Dredge the oysters first in the seasoned flour, then in the egg wash, then in the panko and set aside on a plate.

In a cast-iron pan over high heat, melt ½ cup (125 mL) butter and some bacon drippings, if you have them. Working in batches so as not to crowd the pan, arrange the oysters in a single layer in the hot pan and fry until golden and crispy. Flip, and fry on the other side until browned. Transfer the fried oysters to a paper bag (this soaks off the grease better than paper towels).

Repeat with remaining oysters.

When all the oysters are fried, pull the shells from the oven (they should be warm by now), place the fried oysters back in the shells, and serve on a plate with Come Back Sauce, tartar sauce, or a lemon aioli.

Po'Boy Sandwich

Pan-fry oysters as specified in Pan-Fried Panko-crusted Oysters. Get yourself a nice loaf of bread or bun — a classic French loaf works nicely, but I also like a butter-toasted top slice (New England-style) bun. Spread with Come Back Sauce, stack the fried oysters high up, top with Boston bib lettuce and sliced tomatoes, and enjoy!

Black bean oysters

24 large fresh Fanny Bay "beach" oysters, shucked; liquor reserved
3 tbsp (45 mL) peanut oil
2 large cloves of garlic, coarsely chopped
1 tbsp (15 mL) coarsely chopped peeled fresh gingerroot
2 green onions, coarsely chopped
1 tbsp (15 mL) fermented black beans, rinsed and mashed
1 tbsp (15 mL) soy sauce
1 tbsp (15 mL) rice wine
1 tsp (5 mL) granulated sugar
4 tsp (20 mL) water
2 tsp (10 mL) cornstarch
2 tsp (10 mL) sesame oil
1 to 2 cups (250 to 500 mL) cooked rice
Fresh chives, finely chopped, for garnish

Shuck the 24 oysters into a bowl, and reserve the oyster liquor in a separate bowl.

Spread the empty shells over a baking sheet and place in a 150°F (70°C) oven to warm through.

In a wok over high heat, heat the peanut oil. Add the garlic, ginger, onion, and black beans and heat through.

Add the shucked oysters, toss, and stir-fry until gills start to ruffle, about 1 minute.

Add the soy, rice wine, sugar, and reserved oyster liquor. Toss to combine, then cover, reduce the heat to medium, and let the oysters poach for 2 to 5 minutes (depending on the size of the oysters).

In a small bowl, whisk together the water and cornstarch. Stir in the sesame oil, and fold the mixture into the oyster mixture; toss and heat until the sauce thickens.

Spread the cooked rice over a serving plate. Arrange warmed oyster shells on top. Place one oyster in each shell and spoon over remaining sauce. Garnish chives. Serve immediately.

DESSERT

Salt Water Taffy with Oyster Liquor

2 cups (500 mL) granulated sugar
1 cup (250 mL) light corn syrup
1½ cups (375 mL) oyster liquor, strained
2 tbsp (30 mL) unsalted butter
¾ tsp (3 mL) pure lemon, vanilla, or peppermint extract (your choice)
¼ tsp (1 mL) food coloring (optional)

In a 10-cup (2.5 L) pan over medium-high heat, combine the sugar, corn syrup, salt and strained oyster liquor. Bring to a boil, stirring constantly until the sugar dissolves. Stop stirring and heat mixture until it reaches 255°F (for soft and chewy) or 260 to 265°F (for a hard candy.)

Remove the pan from the heat and mix in the butter, flavoring, and coloring (if using).

Pour mixture into a lightly buttered jelly roll pan or rimmed baking sheet. Let cool just until you are able to handle it with your hands.

Butter your hands and then gather the taffy into a ball and start pulling it. Stretch, pull, fold, and twist — this aerates the taffy, making it lighter and chewy. Continue to pull until it lightens in color and becomes difficult to pull.

Divide taffy into four equal portions. Pull each portion into a ½-inch-thick rope. Cut each rope into 1-inch pieces. Wrap individually in waxed paper. Enjoy!

An Oyster-Loving Chef

When Anthony Bourdain had just published *Kitchen Confidential* some writer friends who'd enjoyed the book wanted to interview Mr. Bourdain. They invited him on an oyster tour of Toronto and asked if I would include one of my oyster knives with the invitation. I offered to go one better, and crafted a custom-made knife from an impression of my own hand. The accompanying note invited the chef to an oyster tasting of five species, including Irish Flats, for which I had a North American exclusive. I also offered to custom-fit a knife to his hand, shucking lesson included. The knife was one of the best I had made. I was looking forward to getting it back for future use. We sent the letter and waited.

It worked. Chef Bourdain arrived at Starfish, sat at the corner of the bar while I shucked oysters for him. I had gotten my hands on four different types of Flats — from France, Maine, B.C. and Ireland. A real feat. Chef enjoyed his oysters. But when it came time to make his knife, he said he was quite happy with the one he had received.

Ah, well. You can't have everything. At least the knife is now in good hands!

Anthony Bourdain (right) with Patrick McMurrary at Starfish

CHAPTER FIVE

OYSTER BARS, OYSTER STARS

*"There is a long marble or hardwood counter between the customer and
the oyster-man, sloping toward the latter. He stands there, opening the
shells with a skill undreamed of by an ordinary man and yet always
with a few cuts showing on his fingers, putting the open oysters carefully,
automatically, on a slab of ice in front of him, while a cat waits with
implacable patience at his ankles for a bit of oyster-beard or a caress."*

— M.F.K. FISHER, *"Consider the Oyster"*

It is true that no two oysters are alike, and the same can be said for
the eating establishments that offer them. Many restaurants will have
oysters on their menu, but true oyster houses, oyster bars, raw bars —
the places that hold the oyster in high regard — will have the word
"oyster" either in their name or prominently displayed on the menu.
The first restaurant I opened was called Starfish Oyster Bed & Grill.
Starfish eat oysters. A simple fact. A simple name. Easy to remember.
(I'd love to take the credit for it, but that belongs to my wife, Alison.)

Enjoying oysters at the Grand Central Oyster Bar, New York

Often, an oyster house or bar is named after the person who owns it (Rodney's, Shaw's, Wright Brothers) or with a nod to its location (Grand Central Oyster Bar, Olympia Oyster House).

To have a good oystery name is one thing, but the interior of an oyster house has to be inviting as well. The layout of the bar is very important: you must be able to see the oysters and the shucker. If the shucker is out of sight in the kitchen, this doesn't necessarily mean that the establishment is "off," but the best places will have the oyster shucker front and center. That way, you know who is opening the oysters — and when.

You should be able to see the rest of the room as well. Part of the "oystering" experience is definitely the social aspect. People with a shared interest — namely, oysters — gather at the bar, almost as if it were planned, and commune over food and drink. Politics, religion, finance, business, legal matters, literature, art, food, drink, sex. It's all there at the oyster bar. Just walk into the light, belly up to the counter, and put yourself in the hands of the shucker.

Plateau de fruits de mer:
A beautiful seafood platter served at many of the best oyster bars

The best bars know the value of a shucker — the "men (and women) with knives" who can handle a fast pace as the orders come in. The good shuckers can share a conversation at the same time; the best will have a few drinks with you and tell a few tales.

Let's take a quick look at my favorite oyster bars, and you'll see how it all adds up — the name, the mood, the menu, the oysters, and the shuckers (of course). But first, a word about etiquette…

An oyster bar can be a daunting place for a first-timer. You can take along friends who know about oysters, but if you decide to go on your own, more power to you!

Here are a few rules to help you relax and enjoy the experience.

1. Sit at the bar.

Whether you're alone or with friends, there's no better place to learn about oysters. It's like sitting at the chef's table in a fancy restaurant — you're in the middle of all the action. The shucker will also help you choose what to drink, and he or she will design a plate of the best oysters in the house to suit your needs. Make friends with your local shucker and you won't go wrong. (*Psst…* It's also a great place to meet other oyster lovers!)

The Oyster Eaters, a caricature by Louis-Léopold Boilly, 1825

2. Check out the oyster menu.

If you're sitting at a table, feel free to come up to the bar and speak to the shucker. Ask for a dozen, made up of different varieties, to start. Then you can choose your favorites for the next round.

3. Be patient.

A good oyster bar shucks oysters to order, to ensure you get the freshest possible product. Sometimes this creates a backlog of orders, especially during peak hours. While you're waiting, have a little bread or order some appetizers from the kitchen. There's no rule that says you have to eat oysters first.

4. Don't cover oysters with a ton of sauce.

Mother Nature planted the seed, a farmer grew it from 18 months to seven years — and you want it to taste like ketchup?! I don't think so. If you like sauce, that's okay, but let the oyster tempt you into enjoying it naked from time to time.

5. Don't cut into a raw oyster on the half-shell before eating.

A large oyster doesn't spend years in the water for you to cut it into small pieces. Choose a smaller oyster instead.

6. The best place to slide the oyster into your mouth is the lip side, not the hinge.

Slide it in and chew it up — this way you will truly experience the merrior, the flavor of that oyster species, from that region, on that day. Each oyster will be slightly different, which makes them so much fun each time.

7. Two-bite chew, and aerate.

Take in some air across the palate. Like in tasting wine, or anything else, the olfactory aids your sense of taste. As you breathe in, you'll notice the flavor changing, developing. Depending on the oyster, you may experience salt, sweet, butter, seaweed, earth, wet stone, or dry tannic copper.

8. Swallow, and think of the oyster some more.

As the flavor develops further, deep as the ocean, and just as refreshing, think about the oyster and where it came from. Now, you can decide to try another one or a dozen.

9. How people stack their shells says a lot about their personality.

If you don't receive a plate or bucket for the shells, I would suggest replacing them upside down on the platter on which they were delivered. Sometimes, when I'm clearing tables, I discover that someone's made a nice design with the empty shells. I applaud this, as it shows that the oyster eater is contemplating the oyster and its existence, not just eating it and throwing out the garbage.

Olympia oysters

10. Like grandma always said, "If you ain't got nothing nice to say about oysters, say nothing at all."

This rules applies, especially when sitting in front to the oyster shucker. Keep it to yourself, thanks. Look around you, these folks are eating this and trying to enjoy their meals. Have you ever tried an oyster? No? Well then, let's chat.

11. Raw oysters aren't for everyone.

Raw oysters contain micro-organisms, plankton, algae, and bacteria that a healthy adult can handle, but they may not sit well if you're young, pregnant, elderly, or have a weakened immune system. When in doubt, call the doctor out. I advise pregnant women to enjoy their oysters cooked until after the baby is born.

12. One more thing…

Call me what you want, but please don't call my oysters fishy. Oysters are fresh, clean, salty, sweet, briny, milky, steely, mineral, chalky, or bitter, with hints of seaweed, driftwood, and mushroom, among other flavors. They are not fishy. Even fresh fish shouldn't taste fishy. To me, it's a derogatory term that should be used only to describe poor-quality seafood. (See Tasting Wheel, page 51.)

A perfect pairing: Champagne and a Galway Bay oyster

THE 80-YEAR-OLD VIRGIN VS. THE OLYMPIA OYSTER

One Friday afternoon at Starfish a couple in their 80s came to the bar. He was gleefully having a dozen oysters. I noticed she wasn't having any. Not a one.

"Will you not have any oysters?" I asked.

"Don't ask her, don't even try. I've tried for years, but she just won't eat them," the man said, enjoying another one.

"My mum is from Cape Breton," the woman said. "She always tried to get me to eat oysters. I never have. I've always hated the look of them, and the size of them. I'm just scared," she explained.

I was shucking a single Olympia, the smallest of the North American oysters, not even the size of a dollar coin. I placed it on a martini glass of crushed ice and seaweed.

"What's that?" she asked, as her husband enjoyed another oyster.

"This is an Olympia oyster. So small, yet most complex in flavor. This oyster just melts on the palate, with ocean sea salt, sweet cream, fresh-cut grass, driftwood, wet stone, and a dry coppery finish, after about a minute." I said. "If you'll excuse me, I have to go to the kitchen for a second."

Upon my return, I noticed the oyster in the martini glass was gone. The fella had tears in his eyes, and the woman was smiling, just beaming.

"I ate the oyster and I liked it!" she was practically shouting. "May I have another?"

"Of course!" I presented her with her own plate of petites. Six oysters later, her husband couldn't believe it.

"To think of all these years," she said, "I never tasted oysters because I was scared and didn't want to. All those years. Today I thought, what the heck, I should try it. My mother won't believe it. I can't wait to tell her!" she said.

"She's still alive?!" I blurted out. "Here's my cell phone. Call her up right now!"

Don't be afraid to try an oyster, or anything for that matter. Lesson learned.

PATRICK'S GUIDE TO
OYSTER ESTABLISHMENTS

Here are some personal favorites that I hope you'll take the time to enjoy, but the world is a big place and there are so many more places than this that you'll stumble upon, both at home and in your travels.

THE UNITED STATES

MASSACHUSETTS

The Clam Box of Ipswich
246 High Street, Ipswich
Tel: 978-356-9707
ipswichma.com/clambox

Go to the Clam Box, my friends, just 30 miles (48 km) north of Boston, and be sure to arrive hungry. This is fried-oyster heaven. There's no raw bar, but a shucker cannot live by raw alone. There's always a lineup but it's well worth the trip! Cash only.

Summer Shack
4 locations: Boston, Cambridge, Mohegan Sun Casino, Logan Airport
summershackrestaurant.com

Renowned New England chef Jasper White has created a very fun place to enjoy lobster, chowder, baked clams, and, of course, an excellent raw bar. Oysters here are served on a bed of ice with an array of sauces.

Neptune Oyster
63 Salem Street, Boston
Tel: 617-742-3474
neptuneoyster.com

At this new, pint-sized oyster bar in downtown Boston, you'll find a dozen or more oysters on any given day, backed by an equally impressive kitchen.

BOSTON

Union Oyster House
41 Union Street
Tel: 617-227-2750
unionoysterhouse.com

The Union is a Mecca for oyster lovers everywhere. They shuck 2,000 to 4,000 oysters a day, sometimes more, so there's no doubt about freshness. And they shuck only one type of oyster at a time — sometimes Chesapeake, some-times Blue Point or Island Creek from Duxbury. The Union has been shucking since 1816, which makes it North America's oldest restaurant. Try to claim one of the six seats in front of the shucker at the original hand-carved soapstone bar. Groups can settle into a booth where the Union's horse stalls once stood.

Anton, Donny, Bob, and the boys have their own unique shucking style. Each man picks up an oyster, inserts a knife into the hinge, then, with confidence and nerves of steel, raises both hands up in one firm, smooth motion and brings the butt of the knife down to hit the board — a cobblestone from old Boston — forcing the oyster onto the knife. Two quick hits and the shells can be sepa-rated with a twist of the wrist. The oyster is then plated without severing the bottom shell. This keeps it alive until it's placed in front of the happy customer.

WASHINGTON, D.C.

Old Ebbitt Oyster Bar & Grill
675 15th Street, NW
Tel: 202-347-4800
ebbitt.com

With its dark wood-paneled walls and leather seats, this restaurant is a haven for politicians, lawyers, and banker types, but there's room to spare for the oyster lovers of the world. Established in 1856, it was a favorite of Presidents Grant, Cleveland, Harding, and Theodore Roosevelt. Oyster stew with five oysters on top is a house specialty, and you'll get great oysters on the half-shell. Home of the Old Ebbitt's Oyster Riot, held on the street in mid-November. Last year, the crew shucked and served 42,000 oysters in two days!

MARYLAND

Nick's Inner Harbor Seafood
1065 South Charles Street, Baltimore
Tel: 410-685-2020
nicksoysterbar.com

This little seafood diner is located at the city market. Not only does Nick's have great shellfish and sandwiches, but it's also the shucking home of two-time U.S. champion George Hastings. If George isn't in, he's probably off catering with his crew of professional oyster shuckers, namely his cousin Vern and brother Bob. It's a family thing.

NEW ORLEANS

Acme Oyster House

724 Iberville Street, French Quarter (and 3 other locations)
Tel: 504-522-5973
acmeoyster.com

This Mecca for oyster lovers in the heart of New Orleans features a long, narrow bar and a great cement trough. Big bags of Apalachicola and Louisiana oysters are dumped into this trough, culled, then shucked onto plates. Belly up to the bar and the shuckers will entertain and feed you. Feeling oysterous? Try for the Wall of Fame. The house record is 50 dozen, by Boyd Bulot. But the kicker is teeny, tiny Sonya "Black Widow" Thomas, a competitive eater, who consumed 52 dozen during Acme's annual Oyster Festival in March 2005. That's 624 oysters — and they're not small, either! Check out the live oyster cam on the website to see what's going on, anytime, all the time.

NEW YORK

Aquagrill
210 Spring Street
Tel: 212-274-0505
aquagrill.com

A beautiful spot to enjoy the oysters. Sit at the bar to take in the ambience, including funky shell artwork produced by the owner's father.

Balthazar Restaurant
80 Spring Street
Tel: 212-965-1785
balthazarny.com

With signature red leather banquettes and a vast 27-foot bar, there's no better place to sample many types of oyster. Order the restaurant's signature multi-tiered *plateau de fruits de mer* — a definite showstopper!

Blue Ribbon Manhattan
97 Sullivan Street
Tel: 212-274-0404
blueribbonrestaurants.com

Loud, fun and open till 4 a.m. every day. Blue Ribbon offers a great selection of oysters and *plateau* of seafood. There is more than enough for land-lovers as well. Go late (or early) and see what local restaurant chefs sup on after their shifts.

NEW YORK

Grand Central Oyster Bar
Grand Central Station
Tel: 212-490-6650
oysterbarny.com

Very few places are as renowned as the Grand Central Oyster Bar
& Restaurant, deep inside the station, with its arched, tiled ceilings
lovingly restored. Even the name implies something larger than life.
When I first started, Grand Central was referred to wherever I went
that had to do with oysters: "These oysters are great, just like the ones
I had at Grand Central."

You can't visit New York without stopping by. Sit in the dining room,
at the sandwich counter, the oyster bar, or the saloon; but you'll find
me at the bar, watching the shuckers deftly open the more than 30
types of oysters on the menu, which changes daily. Steamer pots on
the bar cook up oyster stew or a nice bowl of mussels. This is the place
to feel the history of the oyster and New York all at once. Take your
time. The ability of an oyster bar to sway and calm the New York urban
beast with its sights,
sounds, and flavors has
always intrigued me.
Escape here; many New
Yorkers do. Home of
the Oyster Frenzy and
Grand Central Oyster
Shucking Contest in
late September.

The John Dory Oyster Bar

1196 Broadway at 29th Street

Tel 212-792-9000

thejohndory.com

Chef April Bloomfield's place; enough said. But I must add that this has one of the best oyster happy hours in Manhattan — every day of the working week. The beautiful light-filled room in the Ace Hotel is perfect place to pause for a plate of the oysters, east and west, and a glass of cava.

Mary's Fish Camp

64 Charles Street

Tel: 646-486-2185

marysfishcamp.com

This little eatery in the West Village boasts a decor that reminds many diners of the interior of a bait-and-tackle box: sleek, simple, and functional. There's a countertop and a few tables, but the real hook is the exceptional food — including Malpeques, Wellfleets, and oyster po'boy.

Pearl Oyster Bar

18 Cornelia Street

Tel: 212-691-8211

pearloysterbar.com

Chef and owner Rebecca Charles's Maine-style eatery specializes in the freshest seafood, including oysters, clams, and lobster. Try its reputation-making oyster roll — perfectly-fried oysters stuffed into a top-sliced roll and garnished with tartar sauce. Too bad I can't eat more than one. The *Village Voice* brags that Pearl's also has the best oyster po'boy in town — "You'll want to eat at least one per week!"

CALIFORNIA

Swan Oyster Depot
1517 Polk Street, San Francisco
Tel: 415-673-1101
swanoysterdepot.us

Cash only, no reservations, and constant lineups. This joint is good! A San Fran institution since 1912, the small counter (20 stools or so) serves a few oysters on the half-shell and a great cup of clam chowder. Don't let the lunchtime line dissuade you — it moves fast.

Hog Island Oyster Co.
Ferry Plaza Market, San Francisco
Tel: 415-391-7117
hogislandoysters.com

If you're going out for oysters, why not go to the folks who actually grow them? Hog Island cultivates four to five different oysters and now has a bar of its own, at the north end of the Ferry Building. If you visit the farm, reserve a picnic table so you can enjoy oysters fresh from the water that day. Or spread out a picnic at one of the scenic beaches nearby.

FLORIDA

Dusty's Oyster Bar
16450 Front Beach Road, Panama City Beach
Tel: 850-233-0035

This is the home of three-time U.S. oyster-shucking champion and state title-holder Scotty-O, so you know you can't go wrong. You won't be better entertained, either. This is the place to be when you want to make it "Moister with an Oyster" (ask them to explain!). Grab a beer, go up to the shuckers, and yell "Soociaaall" and see what happens. Then tell them Shucker Paddy sent you.

MAINE

J's Oyster Bar
5 Portland Pier, Portland
Tel: 207-772-4828

This simple room with wood-paneled walls and a central square bar is where the locals come for oysters and conversation. The shucker prepares for the day by shucking more than 500 Chesapeake or Blue Point oysters into a huge mound in the middle of the oyster bed. Not something you see every day! The oysters are then plucked by the service staff and either sent out raw or to the kitchen for cooking. If you're feeling hungry, get the combo of raw and cooked plus a bowlful of the oyster stew.

Fore Street

288 Fore Street, Portland
Tel: 207-775-2717
forestreet.biz

Everything at Fore Street is supplied fresh by local farmers, fishermen, and cheesemakers and is made in-house according to the bounty of the season. Oysters from the Damariscotta River are also available on the daily menu. The applewood-fired ovens give a special taste to every dish.

The glorious Fore Street dining room, close by the harbor in Portland, Maine

CHICAGO

Shaw's Crab House
21 East Hubbard Street
Tel: 312-527-2722
shawscrabhouse.com

This is one of my favorite spots in the world. I discovered it in 1995 when Shaw's called Rodney's to see if we wanted to send a shucker down to their annual Roister with the Oyster Festival in October. Rodney sent me and I got a chance to shuck at the oyster bar — located in the middle of the dining room, with seats all around it. Everyone dines at this 1940s-style house. Shaw's carries a big selection of oysters to enjoy on the half-shell. People stand three deep waiting to get a seat at the bar, so don't be shy.

WASHINGTON STATE

Anthony's Home Port
6135 Seaview Avenue West, Seattle
Tel: 206-783-0780
anthonys.com

Anthony's Restaurants are located throughout the state and all offer a great variety of oysters and fresh fish. But only the Shilshole Bay location has a view of Puget Sound. A Seattle tradition, Anthony's Oyster Games are held on the last Tuesday in March.

Taylor Shellfish Oyster Bars
124 Republican Street, Seattle
Tel: 206-501-4442
taylorshellfishfarms.com

Taylor Shellfish Farms own and operate these three glorious locations in downtown Seattle. Each has its own style. All get rave reviews from diners, and all are worth a visit.

Olympia Oyster House
320 4th Avenue West, Olympia
Tel: 360-753-7000
olympiaoysterhouse.com

Located on the docks, this is the best place to introduce yourself to Olympia oysters, which are difficult to find elsewhere. Be sure to try them raw and pan-fried — the house batter is like no other!

Elliott's Oyster House
1201 Alaskan Way, Pier 56, Seattle
Tel: 206-623-4340
elliottsoysterhouse.com

Watch some of Washington's best shuck through some of the 20-plus varieties available at the long bar. Oysters at Elliott's come with a scoop of frozen mignonette — a tangy sorbet of shallots and champagne — but you'll want to taste them on their own, too. Seafood towers, fresh fish and shellfish, along with events throughout the year, will keep you coming back for more.

The Oyster Bar on Chuckanut Drive
2578 Chuckanut Drive, Bellingham
Tel: 360-766-6185

Chuckanut Drive is one of the most scenic roads I've traveled on, with great views of Puget Sound. Best of all, you can stop at an oyster bar that's grown from a roadside shack in the 1920s to a culinary destination today. The early owners coined the slogan "The oysters that we serve today slept last night in Samish Bay." That says it all.

CANADA

Ontario

Ceílí Cottage

1301 Queen Street East,
Toronto
Tel: 416 406-1301
ceilicottage.com

This is my pub. We serve oysters, naturally, as well as hearty farm-to-table pub fare and Irish and local craft taps and cask. The Cottage hosts The Whiskey Wall, a lovely warm patio, a 120-year-old Cottage room, and a Kilkenny limestone bar built into an old car garage. Irish musicians play live every Tuesday night from 8 to midnight, and we host

Music on Session night at my place,
The Céilí Cottage

happy hours, as well as daily, weekly, and monthly specials and events. This is where, when not in a competition or checking out an oyster farm, you'll find yours truly, Shucker Paddy. Come say "hi" and enjoy some bivalves!

Rodney's Oyster House
469 King Street West, Toronto
Tel: 416-363-8105
rodneysoysterhouse.com

355 10th Avenue SW, Calgary
Tel: 403-460-0026

Rodney's Oyster House in Yaletown (also one in Gastown)
1128 Hamilton Street, Vancouver
Tel: 604-609-9941

With locations in Toronto, Vancouver, Calgary, and their own oyster farm in P.E.I., Rodney's Oyster House is definitely one of the best houses to get a variety of oysters, expertly shucked by Rodney and Eamon Clark, father and son Canadian champion shuckers. P.E.I.-born owner Rodney Clark, an art-school refugee turned fishmonger, is considered a major character in the oyster world. Rodney carries up to

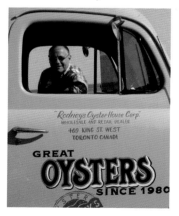

30 different types of oysters from all over North America, and beyond. The shucking crews can answer all of your questions, and they're a treat to watch as the evening unfolds. It's always friendly, always fun, and dining at the bar is highly recommended. The Toronto location is Home of the Ontario Oyster Shucking Championships and the Ontario Opening and Shellfish Festival, held every July.

Oyster Boy

872 Queen Street West, Toronto
Tel: 416-534-3432
oysterboy.ca

Adam Colquhoun and John Petcoff, both excellent shuckers, started Oyster Boy as a catering company. They even offer shucking classes on Saturday afternoons. Their cosy diner features bar-height tables so nobody misses out on the action. The expert staff will help you navigate the 12 different ways Oyster Boy cooks up oysters (keep an eye out for the Oysters Imperial, with baked brie and caviar). The duo proudly features East Coast oysters along with a few choice West Coast varietals.

The Whalesbone Oyster House

430 Bank Street, Ottawa
Tel: 613-231-8569
thewhalesbone.com

Josh Bishop and Peter McCallum, head shuckers at The Bone, will welcome and entertain you with their eclectic style. Enjoy a variety of oysters at the bar and a great supper, including the house Oyster Club Sandwich.

QUEBEC

Joe Beef
2491 Notre Dame Ouest, Montreal
Tel: 514-935-6504

With only 25 seats in the popular restaurant (as reviewers say, "the toughest 25 seats to book in town"), patrons feel like they're part of a lively dinner party — and that's how chef-owners David McMillan and Frederic Morin like it. Head to the bar for a few oysters, mainly from the East Coast, and some great conversation.

Maestro SVP
3615 St. Laurent Boulevard, Montreal
Tel: 514-842-6447
maestrosvp.com

Choose from 12 to 18 different types of oysters from North America and beyond. With its fresh fish, jazz music, and an extensive wine list, this is one of the best places to enjoy your oysters in Montreal.

Au Pied de Cochon
536 Avenue Duluth Est, Montreal
Tel: 514-281-1114
restaurantaupieddecochon.ca

Don't let the name fool you. This popular bistro, which specializes in great hunks of meat, particularly pork, also serves the best-looking seafood towers — oysters included.

PRINCE EDWARD ISLAND

The Claddagh Oyster House
131 Sydney Street, Charlottetown
Tel: 902-892-9661
claddaghoysterhouse.com

The oyster bar in this intimate spot in downtown Charlottetown is set on two levels. This was where you could watch the late, great Canadian Champion oyster shucker and owner John Bil in action. You'll find lots of oysters from the island and From Away as far as B.C. The food is all wonderfully fresh. Liam Dolan, John's partner, has been sighted chair dancing at the Galway Oyster Festival on many occasions. Bil and Dolan also established P.E.I. Shellfish Festival (peishellfish.com) every September. If you're not at the Worlds, you should be here.

Carr's Oyster Bar
Stanley Bridge Harbour
Tel: 902-886-3355

This is the place to have supper on the deck and watch the sun set over New London Bay, home of the Carr's Malpeque oyster. If you're very lucky (or ask nicely), you may get a taste of the family's X/L Fancy oysters. Phyllis and her crew of crack shuckers will open as many oysters as you wish, but save room for one of the best boiled lobsters around. Annual events include the Canadian Championship's pre- and post-parties and Carr's Oyster Bar Amateur Oyster Shucking Competition, held in late August.

MEXICO

Deckman's at Morgos, at Conchas de Peirdra & Agua Mala
deckmans.com
Baja California

The plump Kumiai oysters, which are fantastically complex and briny and grown on the Pacific side of Baja, are served to the delight of patrons at all of expert shucker and chef Drew Deckman's restaurants.

IRELAND

Paddy Burke's — The Oyster Inn
Clarenbridge, County Galway

Tel: +353 (0) 91 96226

paddyburkesgalway.com

Established circa 1650, this dark-walled pub with the large thatched roof sits in the heart of oyster country. "Oysters and Guinness" is the call of the day — particularly in September, during the world-famous Clarenbridge Oyster Festival. Details at clarenbridge.com.

Moran's Oyster Cottage
The Weir, Kilcolgan
10 miles (16 km) south of Galway
(5 min from Clarenbridge)
Tel: 091/796113
moransoystercottage.com

Michael Moran started shucking at a young age and and was in his twenties when, like his father before him, he won the Guinness World Oyster Opening Championship at the Galway Oyster Festival. Moran's has been serving oysters on this spot in the west of Ireland for more than 250 years. The Cottage is so popular, the Morans even have a landing spot for helicopters. One day, during the Races at Lahinch, seven choppers arrived at once wanting to touch down for oysters.

I advise you sit "in the kitchen window" at the front door of the old section, where you can look out across the patio to the Kilcolgan River. Order two pints of Guinness, 12 natives on the half, 12 garlic oysters, and the seafood platter. As the pints are drained, order a second set and then the oysters will arrive. Order the next 12 now because it will take a bit of time. If you arrive at 11:30 a.m. when they open, you'll be able to sell your seat when you're done! Say hello from me.

Sit in the old cottage room, at the front window table and tell them Patrick from Toronto sent you. Your order will be as such: a pint of Guinness, six Kelly's natives on the half-shell, six garlic oysters, and a seafood platter. The second pint will arrive with more oysters as needed.

Aniar Restaurant and Boutique Cookery School
Tartare Café and Wine Bar
56 Lower Dominick Street, Galway City, County Galway
aniarrestaurant.ie

Chef JP McMahon showcases Real Irish Food — oysters and seaweeds at Anair & Tartar. If you're there in September, head to the Galway Oyster Festival, home of the World Championships of Oyster Opening.

Klaw
159 Capel St., North City, Dublin
Tel: +353 1 556 0117
klaw.ie

Squeeze into Klaw — a wee wedge of a point barely 10 feet (3 m) wide — and have them pop open some Harty oysters and Achill Island oysters for a tastey treat.

ENGLAND

LONDON

Wright Brothers
11 Stoney Street, Borough Market
Tel: 0207/4039554
wrightbros.eu.com

This tiny restaurant in the heart of the Borough Market was opened in 2002 by Ben Wright and Robin Hancock, past owners of the Duchy of Cornwall Oyster Farm. Their passion for restoring the oyster to its rightful place in the U.K. culinary consciousness shows in the many local and imported varieties they have on hand — including the signature Helfords, as well as the rare Kumamoto from Humbolt Bay in California, a treat for British oyster fans.

The original Wright Brothers oyster bar in Southwark Market, Borough, London

Sweetings

39 Queen Victoria Street, London
Tel: 0207/2483062

Tucked away in the shadow of St. Paul's Cathedral, this quaint, Old-English institution is open only for lunch. Proprietor Patrick Malloy meets and greets all his customers and arranges where they'll sit for lunch, no matter who they are.

Before you sit down, however, you'll have to partake of a house specialty — a silver tankard of Black Velvet (Champagne and Guinness, if you've never had one). The bartender prepares 10 to 20 before the rush, as it takes time to build them properly.

There are three small bars, each served by a gent in a white jacket and tie. He'll offer you a silver bucket containing Chablis or Muscadet, classic French white wines for fish. Mersey Flat oysters are the house specialty, served six to a plate with a wedge of lemon. Order the house-smoked salmon and eel, too. Each order is written down and handed to a runner, who brings you the plate when it's ready. Finish with the fillet of sole. It arrives at the bar whole, then our man bones it right in front of you with a fork and spoon.

A visit to Sweetings is a delightfully decadent way to start the afternoon — or to spend a four-hour layover at Heathrow, as I did (with pleasure!) several years ago.

Wilton's

55 Jermyn Street, London
Tel: 0207/6299955
wiltons.co.uk

Wilton's, established in 1742, boasts the finest oysters, fish, and game in London. This elegant dining room is also the home of oyster shucker and two-time world champion Sam Tamsanguan, a quiet gentleman who will open oysters for you (without the fanfare normally associated with the Galway Oyster Festival!). Wilton's received its first Royal Warrant in 1884 as Purveyor of Oysters to Queen Victoria, and a second as Purveyors to the Prince of Wales.

SCOTLAND

My ideas of matching oyster and whisky came from a visit to the Isle of Skye, where the Talisker Distillery is only 656 feet (200 m) from the Skye Oyster Farm. Sharing water, ocean, and air makes for a perfect match. There are actually many oyster farms in close proximity to where whiskies are distilled: Islay, Jura, Mull, even Orkney! The Loch Fyne oysters and restaurants throughout Scotland showcase many local oysters. Loch Ryan oysters of Stranraer are the only natives *(O. edulis)* grown in Scotland, and can be "shellebrated" mid-September at the Stranraer Oyster Festival. I'll see you there, and be sure to taste the Rock Oyster Whisky from Douglas Laing.

Rogano

11 Exchange Pl, Glasgow

roganoglasgow.com

Art Deco, painted walls, wood paneling, and mirrors greet you at the front bar and in all the hidden, cozy nooks for champers and shellfish. Opening oysters since 1935.

Ondine

2 George IV Bridge, Edinburgh

ondinerestaurant.co.uk

Upstairs, Ondine has a 14-seat curved oyster bar where you can watch the room and the shuckers at the same time. They showcase oysters from across the UK, not to mention proper Scottish seafood. While perched at the bar, you must sample the langoustines between plates of oysters.

Loch Fyne

Loch Fyne, Clachan, Cairndow

lochfyne.com

Start the car and take the scenic route to Cairndow — home of the Loch Fyne Oyster Bar, Restaurant, and Deli. Oysters, many smoked salmons, local cider, whisky — repeat as often as time permits, and take some seafood from the deli for the ride home. You might want to stop at Loch Fyne Whiskies, the store on the main street in Inveraray, before you leave.

FRANCE

PARIS

La Mascotte
52 Rue des Abbesses, Paris
Tel: 33 101 46 06 28 15
la-mascotte-montmartre.com

Xavier Caille, world champion oyster shucker, can be found enjoying oysters and Champagne here.

I always like to wander around Montparnasse, where you can find:

Le Dome Café
108 Boulevard de Montparnasse, Paris
Tel: 33 101 43 35 25 81
restaurant-ledome.com

Gillardeau is the oyster of choice to find, here as well as a myriad of others!

Le Bar à Huitres
112 Boulevard de
Montparnasse, Paris
Tel: 33 101 43 20 71 01
ww.labarahuitres.com
Enjoy oysters in the open air.

La Coupole
102 boulevard de Montparnasse, Paris
Tel: 33 101 43 20 14 20

Established in 1927, La Coupole at one time was a center of artistic life, frequented by Hemingway, Fitzgerald, Picasso, and Josephine Baker, among others. Today this large brasserie in the heart of Paris still offers tempting *plats de fruits de mer,* oysters, mussels, snails, crab, and lobster. Order Chablis or Champagne and spend the afternoon!

Chez Jacky
Port de Belon (rive droite)
29340 Riéc-sur-Belon
Tel: 0298/06 90 32
chez-jacky.com

The famed Chez Jacky is located at the mouth of the river Belon, in southern Brittany. If you've never been, there is no better place to sample the eponymous Belon oyster. Local oystermen drop off the day's crop to rest in the cement ponds just outside the restaurant. Order up, and the shucker's off to the pond to get you a platter of memorable Flats. According to the *International Herald Tribune,* this is "the quintessential waterside fish restaurant."

Don't forget Cafe Turin when in Nice, and just go to Marennes Orleon and stay in a Fisherman's Oyster Shack overnight.

HOLLAND

de Oesterbar
Leidseplein 10, 1017 Pt Amsterdam
Tel: 020 623 2988
oesterbar.nl

Look for the Smit & Smit land-based cultured oysters at this oyster bar in Amsterdam.

BELGIUM

Belga Queen
Rus fosse aux loups 32, Brussels
Tel: 32 (0)2 217 2187
belgaqueen.be

Once a bank, this lush gallery-like setting is the perfect place to experience any of the fine varieties offered here.

ESTONIA

Tallink Spa and Conference Hotel
Sadama 11a, 10111 Tallinn, Estonia
Tel: 372 630 1000
tallinkhotels.com

You can find three-time world champion oyster shucker Anti Lepik moonlighting as executive chef at the Tallink Aqua Spa. When he's not there, he's organizing the national championships at Restaurant Nero in Tallinn, Estonia.

SWEDEN AND NORWAY

Klemmings Ostron
Grebbestad, Bohülsan, Sweden
Tel: 46 (0) 762 736623
klemmingsostron.com

Klemmings was founded twenty-five years ago by Peter and Bengt Klemming. They produce *O. edulis* and *C. Viginica* for leading Nordic restaurants and cafés. Between Gothenburg and Oslo by the Fjälbacka achipelago, Klemmings is the destination for oyster aficionados. Peter met his wife at Grebbestad and their daughter Lotta has been raised on and under the water. "It's heavy, dirty and sometimes dangerous work for a young woman," she says. "But I wanted to prove myself. Not to speak of gender, but it's a fact." A brief visit to their site will direct you to the best and most interesting restaurants in that part of the world. Klemmings organizes oyster diving safaris, and they supply the oyster academy at the nearby TanumStrand. Definitely worth the trip to Sweden!

Lotta Klemming, harvesting the best Swedish oysters by hand
on the shore at her family's oyster farm

SPAIN — GALICIA

Oysters are the gastronomic pearl of Vigo's estuary. Grown in Arcade, every morning they're transported directly from the beds to Pescadería Street, the one that everyone in Vigo calls *Calle de las Ostras* (Oyster Street). Grown here since Roman times, these oysters are sold every day by four oyster sellers in the Old Town.

SINGAPORE

Greenwood Fish Market
Various restaurants and locations

In 2005 I had the pleasure of shucking at Canadiana Raw Bar at the Marina Mandarin in Singapore. Back then the local oyster was the Lighthouse from Malaysia — plump, salty, and pine-like woodyness, a mangrove oyster! Today seafarmers at Ubin farms provide Pacific

C. gigas oysters delivered sea to table on the same day, anywhere in Singapore. Look for them and other great varieties of oysters and shellfish at any of the fine Greenwood Fish Market establishments.

CHINA

I've been to China several times, and in 2010 broke my first Guinness Record of 33 oysters per minute to 38 oysters per minute on CCTV in Beijing. At the time my friend and fellow oyster fan Rudy Guo showed me several cities, and has since created several great places to enjoy a vast array of oysters from all corners of the globe. China hosts the China Shuck Off World Cup in four cities annually.

BEIJING

C Pearl, Beijing and Fuzhou
The Plump Oyster, Shanghai

Owner Rudy Guo went to culinary school in Toronto, and always wanted to bring the Western oyster bar concept to China. He brought me over a couple of times to showcase oysters in a Western light, shucked on the bar, served with Champagne and sauces. With fresh imports from all across the globe, Rudy offers a great oyster list, changing with each shipment. Look forward to The Annual International Shuck Off event in May, where top shuckers are brought in to compete, and serve oysters to all who attend!

HONG KONG

Open Oyster
Shop 56, G/F South Seas Centre, 75 Mody Road, Tsim Cha Tsui
Tel: 852 2366 3808

There were only one or two places to have oysters when I was last in Hong Kong some 10 years ago, now there are dozens to choose from. After a day adventuring around Hong Kong, and visiting the fish shacks at Llama Island, Open Oyster is the perfect place to enjoy a whack of oysters from around the world.

JAPAN

Over 30 different oysters are grown around Japan. Hokkaido features the Kakiemon which is available year-round due to the cool, temperate waters. Oysters can also be found in Miagi, Hiroshima, Saga, Nagasaki and, of course, Kumamoto. Find a great variety at Tokyo's Ota Market, Shinichi Yamada of Yamakosa.

The Tokyo Oyster Bar
141-0022 Tokyo, Shinagawa, Higashigotanda
Tel: 81 3 3280 3336

The Tokyo Oyster bar has beed shuckin' around since 1999 and draws a large crowd to watch their fast shuckers at work.

The Oyster Bar

4F atre Shinagawa, 2-18-1 Konan, Minaot-ku, Tokyo
Tel: 03 6717 0932
oysrwe bartokyo.com

The popularity of the oyster lead to the opening of an oyster bar modeled after the the oyster bar of Grand Central Station, New York City. The Grand Central Oyster Bar is one of the most renowned restaurants in the United States and is now also found, with similar ambiance to the original location, in Shinagawa Terminal Station.

AUSTRALIA

Coffin Bay Oysters

9 Martindale Street, Coffin Bay
Tel: 04 2826 1805

Take a tour and enjoy freshly shucked oysters right from the sea.

Coffin Bay Tours

Beachcomber Cafe, 114 Esplanade
Tel: 61(0) 488139 032

Why go to a regular oyster bar, like everyone else? Don the hip waders and get right into the water at Coffin Bay's wade-in oyster bar and farm tour.

The Sydney Cove Oyster Bar

Tel: 02 9247 2937

sydneycoveoysterbar.com

What better place to find Sydney rock oysters than on the waterside patio at The Sydney Cove Oyster Bar. Look for McAsh and Clyde River oysters. The location is perfect for growing year-round oysters with a peak season of November to May.

TASMANIA

Get Shucked

Lease 204, 1735 Bruny Island Main Road

Bruny Island

Tel: 0439 303 597

getshucked.com/au

If you are going to go south, go all the way to the Get Shucked oyster farm and bar that offers bay-to-bar dining of their home-grown oysters from Bruny Island.

NEW ZEALAND

The New Zealand Oyster Trail
Yes, it's for real. Do it. And enjoy.

Bluff Oyster and Food Festival
Bluff, New Zealand
bluffoysterfest.co.nz

One of the rarest oysters in the world, with a short season of March to August, this oyster is "shellabrated" in May at the Bluff Oyster Fest.

Oyster Cove
8 Ward Parade, Bluff 9814
Tel: 64 3 212 8855
oystercove.co.nz

Enjoy your oysters with a 180-degree view of Ruapuki, Dog, and Stewart Island at Oyster Cove.

Oyster Trails
Around the globe

The popularity of oysters has exploded across the globe. Not only are there more farmers growing these shells, oyster fans want to go visit, see, and taste the oyster fresh from the water! Oyster Trails offer mini, local tours where you can source and discover the hidden ocean gems. Alabama, Virginia, Jersey (UK), Nova Scotia, British Columbia, and New Zealand, to name a few, offer online maps and discovery routes. Take a road trip!

CHAPTER SIX

THE ART OF SHUCKING

In the late nineteenth century and the early years of the twentieth century, oyster shuckers in American Eastern seaboard canning factories were largely women and young children (even newly freed slaves, after the end of the American Civil War) who labored long hours for low wages in poor working conditions. They were paid by the gallon — so the more they shucked, the more they earned. Today, the shucking plants of the East and West coasts are state-of-the-art operations, but the "shuck more, earn more" rule still applies. On a recent visit to the Olympia Oyster Company in Washington State, I had an opportunity to see the shucking room in action.

The shuckers work in two rows on either side of a large central hopper that deposits oysters to each shucking station. Their technique is more forceful than mine, since they're dealing with the big beach oysters of the Pacific, but they are remarkably fast — and very efficient. I witnessed one shucker "bang" into the hinge by placing the oyster onto the knife and hitting the butt of the knife on the work table.

With two sharp taps, the knife was in, the bottom muscle cut, the shells torn apart, and the meat cut off the top shell. All done with such speed that I could hardly register the individual actions!

The oyster meat goes into a stainless-steel gallon container, and the shells are whisked away on a conveyor belt to an awaiting bin, outside the warehouse, to be processed later. When the shuckers fill their gallon containers, they pass them to the grader, who inspects the oysters for quality before packing. For each gallon filled, a token is issued. At the end of the day, the tokens are traded in for cash at the main office. At the Olympia Oyster Company, a journeyman shucker can easily fill 30 gallons during a seven-hour shift. That translates into roughly $150 a day — or more, depending on speed.

Shuckers have also plied their trade in taverns, restaurants, and fancy dining rooms with oysters on the menu, but their work was usually done in the kitchen and away from watchful eyes. Now, with the rise of celebrity chefs and with more discerning restaurant-goers who want to know where their food comes from and how it's prepared, professional shuckers are finally getting the recognition they deserve. Today, oyster lovers look for specialty restaurants where they can watch their dinner being freshly prepared at the bar while engaging in repartee with the shucker. A busy oyster bar full of impatient customers is the best place to hone one's skill. It's shuck or be shucked. The best rise to the top and just keep getting better with practice.

Eventually, someone will comment on how slow or fast the shucker works — and then the glove comes off...

CHEF GORDON RAMSAY AND SHUCKER PADDY GO FOR THE *GUINNESS*

One Friday night while working the bar, I received a call from Los Angeles. It was *The F Word*. Gordon Ramsay wanted to challenge Guinness holders to break their records live on the show.

"Do you think you could teach Gordon to get close to breaking your record of opening 38 oysters a minute?" the producer asked.

"Well, Chef's a leftie, so I'll be teaching backwards."

"Yes, but do you think he could beat your record?"

"Chef could get close. He could open 30 to 38 oysters, but I'll open 44 in that minute."

"You're hired."

The battle took place on the Santa Monica Pier at 7 a.m. We would have three chances to break the record. Chef Ramsay is a real professional who has ultimate respect for food and therefore the oyster.

Gordon Ramsay and Patrick McMurray chatting on the pier

On the first round, I shucked 35 oysters. The second time always feels slower than the first. By then, oysters are the second string, not as good as the first round. I shucked 36, so we had to do it again. We set the third string of oysters, widening the space between them.

Oysters must be edible after the contest to qualify for the *Guinness Records,* as one of the rules specifies that there be no food wastage. After scrutinizing the oysters on the third and final attempt, two of mine were discounted as they were still attached. However, I successfully opened 39 oysters, creating a new world record, 39 oysters opened in one minute!

Thank you, Chef, for the opportunity. And that is, as they say, that. There's more to this story, but that's for another time, across the bar at The Ceílí.

LET THE CONTEST BEGIN!

The most common type of oyster contest is shucking for speed, or Pop and Drop — removing the top shell and moving on. In 2002, I landed in the Guinness Book of World Records for shucking 33 oysters in 1 minute. (I used Aspy Bays from Nova Scotia, one of the easiest oysters to open.)

Jim Red, a shucker at the Union Oyster House in Boston, argues that speed is fine and dandy, "but you don't work for three minutes a day, do you? Give me 500 oysters and then we'll see just how good you are!" I'm intrigued by this one. Though it wouldn't be as exciting as a speed contest, I'm game to try, after we find some way to make use of all those shucked oysters. Any volunteers?

Most contests I have entered follow the same basic rules: open a specified number of oysters, sever the meat from the bottom shell and present the oysters on a tray to a judge within a prescribed time. At the Guinness World Oyster Opening Championships (part of the Galway International Oyster Festival, held in September), competitors must open 30 Galway Flats. At the Canadian Oyster Shucking Championships in Tyne Valley, P.E.I., it's 18 Malpeques. Competitors at the U.S. Nationals in St. Mary's, Virginia, shuck 24 Chesapeake Bay oysters. And contestants at Anthony's Oyster Games in Seattle shuck 12 each of the five oyster species. Now that's a contest!

How you open the oyster during competition is up to you. Table top, in your hand, any method is fine as long as you shuck the oysters, present them on a tray, then step back from the table and tap a signal or ring a bell to indicate you're finished. (And no touching the tray once you're done, or you may be disqualified.) Speed kills, even when dealing with oysters, and shucking too quickly has occasionally killed my chances of winning. Clean oysters, properly presented, will triumph every time.

BLADE RUNNERS

The adage "You're only as good as the tools you use" rings true in the world of the oyster shucker. A knife is an integral part of the shucker's life and spirit. Shucker and knife are rarely separated.

Every shucker has a special knife — a certain configuration of blade and handle, sharp or dull, hand-polished or grinder-finished — that works magic on an oyster shell. It's customized with tape, putty, and bandages according to fashion, and tuned on a diamond or ceramic whetstone. Some shuckers will use up to 10 different knives for the various types of oysters; others, just one.

When I first started shucking, I used the simple and versatile Richards oyster knife. Today, my knife is made by Swissmar, available globally, with its signature bright yellow pistol-grip and notch blade. It gets me through 284,862 oysters — a lifetime for most people, but just two years for me (see endpages, centre knife.)

A Shanghai shucker at his stall in the local market

Swedish champion Per Olofsson owns about 10 different hand-forged steel blades. (I'm convinced he has a personal knife-maker toiling somewhere in the backwoods of Sweden!) His favorite has a flat back and a wide, curved blade that often matches the shell he's opening, so he can sever the meat with just one stroke. A notch the width of a finger creates a point at the hilt that takes the top off cleanly.

Per's famous colleague Deiter Berner has invented a double-ended knife. The bottom blade is curved like a spoon, which allows him to slip under the oyster for a closer cut of the adductor muscle.

At my first Galway championships, I was astounded to learn that the Irish champion shucker Michael Kelly uses an old steak knife ground down, with the handle taped up for grip and size. Another Irish champion, Michael Moran, fashioned his blade from a 12-inch (30 cm) chef's knife. The steel is thick and sturdy, and the handle is taped for grip and comfort. Like most Europeans, he pushes his knife through the oyster's hinge, cuts the top, then finishes the bottom.

While you may admire a shucker's favorite knife, please don't ask to borrow it — especially just before competition season starts. I once lent my knife to a young novice (who's now a great shucker, by the way). Of course, she got stuck in an extra-large oyster while flexing the blade the wrong way. When she raised her head, the knife snapped off at the hilt. She was devastated, and so was I. I realized then that I shouldn't lend my good knife because if it's going to break, I should be the one holding it.

If you're serious about shucking, you may find something among the ready-made knives that are available from various companies. Be sure to get the blade ground to an appropriate shape (most knife companies produce stock dull blades to be extra-safe). And get the tip ground to a soft point, so you can get it into the shell with minimal force.

Laguiole: With its ram's-horn handle, hand-forged steel blade, and brass fittings, this elegant knife is dead sexy. It even comes in a wooden box with a board. Although this is the most beautiful oyster knife made, it is designed only for the French style of side, or lip, opening. The blade is very sharp and pointed, which will get you through the thinner shell up front — but if you try at the hinge, chances are you'll twist the blade.

A selection of Per Olofsson's knives.

Dexter-russell: This Massachusetts company is the oldest and largest maker of professional knives in the United States. It produces over a dozen oyster knives, in classic blade and handle configurations — including Providence, Boston, New Haven, and Galveston. A personal favorite is the 4-inch (10 cm) S122 Boston pattern.

Ostero: Xavier Caille of Paris loves this French manufacturer of oyster knives. He uses different blades on different types of oysters, but finds that the Master Ecailler Knife No.8 is the best overall. Xavier gave me one, just because I import Spéciales Gillardeau oysters (his favorite), and the Ostero No.8 is the only knife worthy of using on such a wonderful oyster! So says Xavier, so shall it be done! The handle is made of Bubinga wood and gets a little sticky when wet. The stainless steel blade is wide and curved, designed for side entry only. If you try to use this knife in the hinge, it will twist.

Richards: This economical entry-level knife is fun to experiment with. Just don't put it in the dishwasher or the blade will rust. Hand-wash and keep it dry, and the knife will last for years. Back at Rodney's, we used to go through boxloads of these knives.

ANATOMY OF A WINNER

I've been opening oysters for over 25 years now, and compete in several contests every year. The thrill of the competition is what drives me to strive for speed, consistency — and for that elusive perfect oyster. The nervous anticipation, the roar of the crowd, are all part of the event, but I know I need to remain focused to win a shucking contest. I've seen many excellent competitors thrown off their game by a noisy crowd. After one contest, friends told me that five people had tried to talk to me, cheer me on, and give me a high five, but I hadn't noticed. They had been part of the blur of color and motion in my peripheral vision as I concentrated on the table and the oysters in front of me.

Technique, visualization, biomechanics, ergodynamics … these are useful bits of information I picked up while attending the University of Toronto's Faculty of Physical and Health Education years ago. And while oyster shucking wasn't one of the degree requirements for coaching, the same theories can be applied at the competition table.

Let's start with the layout. I arrange the oysters in a columned-fan pattern on my right-hand side so they won't jumble around when I grab for them. Each one is in proper alignment with my hand, so when I place the oyster on the board, it is positioned correctly. And the oysters are located within a radius equal to my arm reach (you waste time if you have to reach too far). Once the oysters are laid out in front of me, my hands go above my head, ready for the call.

3, 2, 1, GO! Generally, I move on the count of 1, and hit the oyster on GO. This is not a false start, but a fast one, which took a few years to perfect. The Canadian Championships are tougher because Roderick, the organizer, changes his call every year. Sometimes it's really fast, sometimes he calls it slowly—and sometimes he doesn't say "GO." It changes every year, sometimes during the contest.

World champion Michael Moran — game ready

Then, the technique. The first few oysters are the toughest. I start with the most difficult-looking shells so I can take my time and find my rhythm. I grasp the oyster with my left hand, knife blade on left thumb, into the hinge, apply pressure, pry with the oyster-hand's index finger, torque down, sweep across the meat, touch the adductor muscle with the knife, pop off the shell, throw the shell, sweep for grit with my right knife-hand, turn 180 degrees with the left, hold tight, two-cut the adductor, make sure it's clean and three-cut if necessary while I glance at the next oyster, place the last one with the left hand, pick up the next oyster with my right hand, place it on the board, check the finished oyster for any meat out of the shell, and grasp the oyster with the left hand, knife on thumb. That's 4.77 seconds.

Repeat 18 times. Breathe after four oysters. Slow and steady breathing keeps you on track. When I'm done, I raise my hands and call TIME to stop the clock.

I call out TIME loudly now, for one reason. In 1999, I was at Anthony's Oyster Olympics (in Seattle), a fantastic team contest of shucking, oyster identification, and wine tasting. The oyster shucking consisted of five species, 12 of each. I was one of 25 shuckers, all of whom shucked at the same time. Interesting, but a logistical nightmare, since you also need 25 timers and an appropriate number of judges. On my second set of five plates, I finished quickly, raised my hands, and looked down at the oysters to see that my timer was chatting with the timer next to him! I shouted TIME three to five seconds later, which,

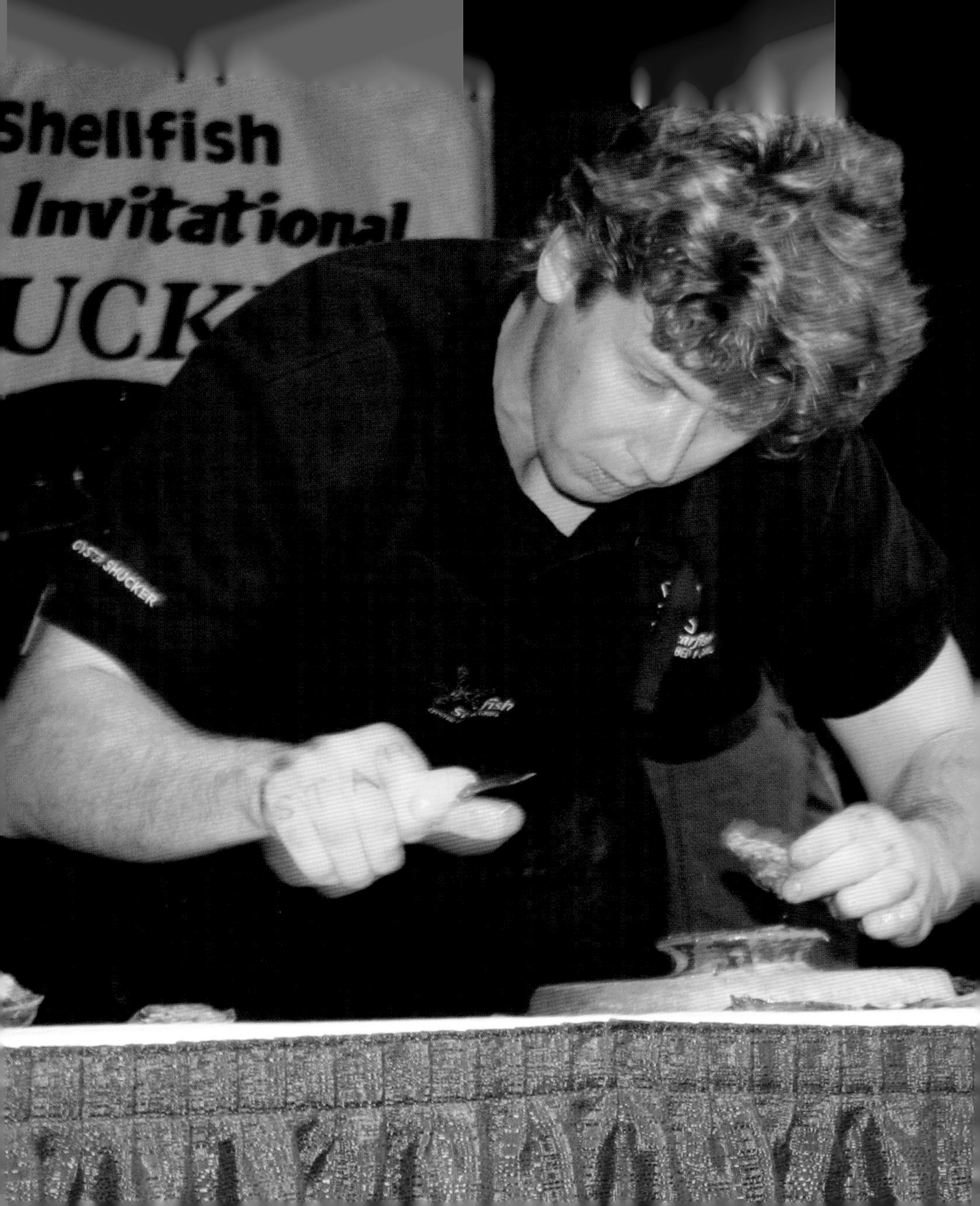
Shellfish
Invitational

in a contest, can cost you one placing or more. Luckily, the timer clued in that I might be a bit quicker than most and paid attention for the rest of the contest. In the end, I came in second, and the team won first overall. (We got kicked out of three bars after that victory!)

Another option to stop time is to tap the table; at the Worlds in Galway, we are required to ring a little brass bell. But when you're pumped up on adrenaline, things can go wrong. One year, at the Canadian Championships in Tyne Valley, as I finished my plate, my knife-hand came down to tap the table, hitting it so hard that the tray and the neatly shucked oysters jumped into the air several inches. I watched in horror as the shells fell back into the tray as if in slow motion, landing in a jumbled pile. Needless to say, I lost that gig.

Light tap, arms up, shout TIME, exit stage right.

Next, the presentation. When presenting the finished tray, my oysters are placed a thumb-width apart so they won't dislodge their neighbor or leave any grit. Bivalves at Ontario competitions are presented on ice, so they sit nicely and don't move. At the Canadian and World competitions, they're placed on a square tray with nothing underneath. This is tricky because the oysters may rock and fall out of their shell. One solution is to line the tray with a damp terrycloth bar towel, which supports the shells and keeps the oysters steady while the timers move the full tray to the judging table.

At the Ontario competition, chez Rodney's Oyster House in Toronto, four shuckers compete at a time and cheering is encouraged, the louder the better. After each heat, the judges inspect the shucked oysters

---

In the zone

while the next group prepares its station. Penalty points are given for grit, cuts in the meat, meat not severed, a broken shell, oysters out of their shell, or blood. You can cut yourself all you want during a shucking competition — just don't bleed on the oysters!

The penalty points are added to the flat time, and the result determines your position.

With the faster shuckers setting the pace, I've noticed that the times get progressively faster, though the oysters don't necessarily end up cleaner. The crowd loves the action and pushes you on. A good shucker will block out the noise and concentrate on the task at hand.

And finally: the results. Awaiting the results is the hardest part of the contest for me — I'm always expecting the judges to announce: "In tenth place, Patrick McMurray." To soften the blow, I whisper my name: In ninth place, Patrick McMurray; in eighth place … and so on.

Once we get to the top three, there's a pause as the judges announce the Best Presentation (lowest number of penalty points) and Fastest Knife (fastest knife off the table). These trophies usually go to someone in the top three. If you win both, you're guaranteed first place, but nobody has accomplished this yet. It's one of my personal goals.

CHAMPIONSHIP TECHNIQUES AROUND THE WORLD

The art of getting good at anything is to watch and analyze how others do the same job. There are many ways to shuck an oyster, and these are the best in the world.

Bernard Gauthier
France
World Champion 1990, 1992, 1994, 1997

Bernard is the fastest in the world almost every time he competes. His average time off the table for 30 Irish Flats is two minutes. (Five of the best shuckers are in the 2.5-minute zone, and most will finish their tray in just over three minutes.) C'est vite ou quoi?! Bernard uses the French side-opening technique. He inserts his knife at the side, closest to the adductor muscle, and, in one motion, severs the muscle, pulls back on the top shell, removing it, then cleans the bottom with a flick of the wrist.

In 1997, on my second trip to the Worlds in Galway, I came in second-fastest off the table — 30 seconds behind Bernard, and 30 seconds faster than the rest of the pack. Since Bernard did not speak English, his wife came over to me to tell me how impressed Bernard had been with my speed that day. And then she presented me with his traditional Oysterman's Jacket: a royal blue ¾-length zip-front tunic, with a red "sailor's" collar/cape. I still have it in my collection today.

(In the oyster shucker's world, this is like Wayne Gretzky skating over and giving you the jersey off his back!)

Deiter Berner
Sweden
World Champion 1998, 2003

Deiter has developed one of the most interesting, and effective, ways of opening an oyster. He uses a modified chef's knife — the top blade has one sharp edge, and the bottom blade is curved to match the curve of the oyster shell.

In competition, Deiter places his oysters on his left-hand side, upside down, in rows, hinges pointing away from him. He then cups his left hand and pops an oyster into his palm, perfectly positioned in his hand, with the hinge to his fingers. The top blade is positioned between his fingertips and the hinge. Once the blade is along the hinge, Deiter closes his fist, effectively pushing the knife through the hinge. Once the knife is in, the right-hand thumb grasps the top shell with the blade, removes it with a twist and drops the shell at his feet. In this position, the top blade is away from the oyster, exposing the bottom curved blade, which is now inserted under the adductor. With a turn of both wrists, he severs the bottom muscle!

The knife hand then places the oyster on the presentation tray, while the cupped hand pops up another oyster. Trust me, it's as difficult as it sounds. But it's also beautifully, massively fluid, with no wasted motion — which is the name of the game in shucking! It also helps to have really big hands, like Deiter's. And you know what they say…. Big hands … big gloves!

Murph G. Murphy was the first of our little Toronto clan of shuckers to make it to the World Championships in 1994. We would gather around the oyster bar as he spun wonderful stories of oysters, and dancing, and merriment, and of a Swedish guy's double-ended oyster knife.

In 1996, it was my turn to vie for the title in Galway, and I met Deiter Berner in the marquee on the Claddagh. We traded stories of oysters, he showed me his technique, then ran through what we were expected to do in the competition and how to lay out the oysters in the tray. When the day was over, I had come in third, and Deiter presented me with his knife. I don't know which was the greater honor. Probably, his knife.

Per Olofsson
Sweden
World Champion 2000

Although Per shucks in his hands, his technique is very different from Deiter's. Per's knife has one sharp edge to it, with a deep curve at the top, a short notch at the hilt and a flat spine for pushing the knife. Per holds the oyster in his left hand, hinge to his fingertips, and, with the knife, enters the oyster through the hinge using the point at the notch.

Once the knife is set, he then pushes the blade through the hinge and pulls the shell off with his thumb, shell to his feet. With the deep curve of the top of the blade, Per then severs the bottom of the adductor muscle and moves for the next oyster. Another blazing-fast technique — but try it with a duller knife, a pair of gloves, and Per looking over your shoulder to make sure all goes well!

George Hastings
United States
World Championships 2006 — 2nd place
U.S. Champion, 1999, 2003

George loves to talk and spin a few yarns while he shucks, so he has developed an effective combo technique for opening oysters. He puts his oyster on the board and cracks the hinge with his right hand. While the knife is in the oyster, he cuts the bottom adductor first. Then, with a twist, he takes the top shell off — with the oyster attached! The shell in his hand, he severs the muscle and presents the plump morsel on the top shell. The oyster looks much fatter in this position, and the top shell prevents the oyster from rocking around on the platter.

Chopper Young
United States
World Champion 2008
U.S. Champion 2007, 2008, 2013

If you are fortunate enough to attend any contest with Chopper on the bill, you're in for a treat! Chop is one of the fastest knives I've ever seen. He's modified a plain old dinner knife by shaping the blade and thinning the kerf so that the metal can slide into the thinnest of shells as he shucks in his hand. Chop enters at the hinge and, with a twist and forward stroke, has the top shell flying forward. In one fluid movement, as his hand comes back from launching the top shell, he slices the adductor muscle off the bottom shell, then places the lovely oyster on the tray. Do not blink, or you'll miss it. I had to use super slow-motion film to figure it out!

Michael Moran
Ireland
World Champion 2006

Young Michael Moran has been oystering with his father for most of his twenty-three years. Many children will tell you they don't want to grow up to be their parents. Not so with Michael, who is itching to return to the family business after a stint in the banking world in Dublin. "Oysters and restaurants… It's in your blood," he confided to me last year during the Worlds. And being the next of seven generations, I expect it's in his blood more than most.

In competition, Michael uses a modified chef's knife, cut down to about 4 inches (10 cm) from the hilt, with a stocky, curved blade shaped to finish the bottom shell efficiently. He will pick up the oyster with his (right) knife hand and place it into his left, hinge toward his fingertips. Then he brings the knife to the hinge, wraps the fingers of his left hand around the spine of the knife and "pushes" the blade through. With a little wiggle on the right, he pops off the top shell, cuts the adductor muscle and scrapes the meat off the shell. One at a time, the shells are placed in perfect, straight lines until all thirty are done — in about 2.5 minutes!

Maria Petersen
Norway
Norwegian Oyster Battle, First Place, 2017

Nordic champion shucker Maria uses the Helgass single blade technique to quickly and cleanly present oysters. A second generation shucker, Maria may have learned some tips and techniques from her champion father Heini Peterson, chef and owner of Vintage Kitchen in Oslo. Maria also organizes Norwegian Oyster Battle each August. Maria's technique won her Cleanest Plate in Galway 2017 — she is the next generation rising!

Deborah Pratt
USA

World Championships 1997 — 2nd Place
U.S. Champion, 1991, 1992, 1997

I first met Deborah Pratt in 1997, at the World Championships in Galway. Salt of the earth friendly, Deborah showed me her four-time US Champion "bill shucking technique". A quick stab through the front of the shell, severing the muscle with a flick of the wrist, snapping the bottom shell off and presenting her oysters on the top shell. Fat, plump, nick free, and on the flat top shell, Deborah's oysters don't rock around in the Galway contest tray. Deborah came second in the World that year, adding to her many US and Virginia championships — and she's #1 in my thoughts of fantastic personable shuckers!

Deborah Pratt, champion shucker, rules Virginia from the half shell

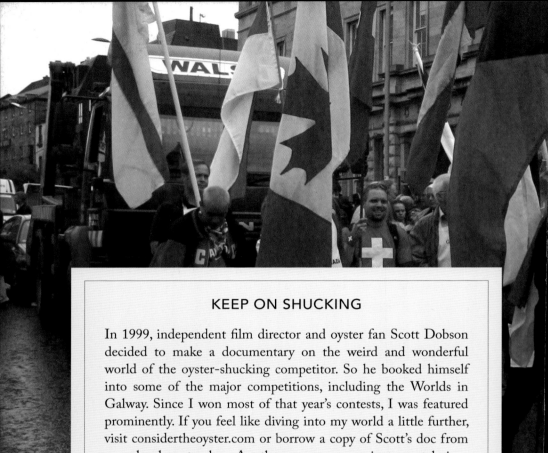

KEEP ON SHUCKING

In 1999, independent film director and oyster fan Scott Dobson decided to make a documentary on the weird and wonderful world of the oyster-shucking competitor. So he booked himself into some of the major competitions, including the Worlds in Galway. Since I won most of that year's contests, I was featured prominently. If you feel like diving into my world a little further, visit considertheoyster.com or borrow a copy of Scott's doc from your local oyster bar. Another gorgeous movie to watch is a documentary about a Japanese-American family that has been oyster farming for generations. *Ebb and Flow*, by Shelly Solomon. The movie takes you on a beautiful journey that explains the moniker transformation of the Japanese oyster, now well-loved and known as the Pacific oyster.

ACKNOWLEDGMENTS

With Thanks

This book took as long to produce as it takes an oyster to produce a pearl. My pearls are Alison, Leiden and Spencer. Together we're the PALS, and I'm grateful for your love and support (and for putting up with me while I was shucking around!). Special thanks to my Mom and Dad, who inspired me with travel, good food, art, paper, antiques and teaching.

I am indebted to Rodney Thomas Clark for introducing me to the oyster and to P.E.I. — and for putting the fun back into dining in Toronto.

— PATRICK McMURRAY

SELECTED BIBLIOGRAPHY

DeMers, John & Jaeger Andrew. *Oysters*. Berkeley: Celestial Arts, 1999.

Fisher, M.F.K. *Consider the Oyster*. New York: North Point Press, a division of Farrar, Straus and Giroux, 1954.

Hilton, Lisa. "Go on, you know you want it," *The Observer*, September 14, 2003.

Kurlansky, Mark. *The Big Oyster*. London: Jonathan Cape, 2006.

Neild, John. The English, *The French and The Oyster*. London: Quiller Press, 1955.

Stott, Rebecca. *Oyster*. London: Reaktion Books, 2004.

Yonge, C.M. *Oysters*. London: Willmer Brothers & Haream Ltd., Birkenhead for Collins Clear Type Press. 1960.

PICTURE CREDITS

All images are by Patrick McMurray or from his collection unless otherwise noted.

Cover: Tauqir Shah/ bigshahfilms.com

Endpapers: Admir Alimajstorovic/ Addy Photographic

2–3: By kind permission of the Duchy of Cornwall Oyster Farm.

3 (inset): Diana Sullada.

4–5: *The Oyster Gatherers of Cancale* by John Singer Sargent. The Corcoran Gallery of Art/ CORBIS.

9: By kind permission, The Wright Brothers, Borough, London.

11: By kind permission of The Oyster Bar, Grand Central Terminal.

12: Bettmann/CORBIS.

24–25: Maximillian Stock Ltd/ photocuisine/ CORBIS.

25: Nicoloso/photocuisine/CORBIS.

38: Owen Franken/CORBIS.

42: Nik Wheeler/CORBIS.

46–47: By kind permission of the Duchy of Cornwall Oyster Farm.

51: Art by Gregory Kit.

55: James L. Amos/CORBIS.

60: By kind permission, Rodney's Oyster House.

75: Jerry Braasch/CORBIS.

67: Owen Franken/CORBIS.

71: Jacqui Hurst/CORBIS.

88: Michelle Garrett/CORBIS.

112: James L. Amos/CORBIS.

100–101: Hulton-Deutsch Collection/CORBIS.

86: C. Murtin/photocuisine/ CORBIS.

91–93: Rob Riley.

94: Owen Franken/CORBIS.

118: Bo Zaunders/CORBIS.

106–107: Roger Viollet/Getty Images.

109, 110, 111: Admir Alimajstorovic/ Addy Photographic.

109: Owen Franken/CORBIS.

110: Jeremy Bemberon/Sygma/ CORBIS.

114: National Gallery Collection. By kind permission of the Trustees of the National Gallery, London/CORBIS.

120: Massimo Borchi/Atlantide Phototravel/CORBIS.

123: Justin Guariglia/CORBIS.

116–117: By kind permission of John McCabe.

136: Brittany Ross.

141: Bettmann/CORBIS.

147, 204: Peter Schafrick Photography.

151: Mark L. Stephenson/CORBIS.

160: By kind permission of Wright Brothers, Borough, London.

174: Rita Maas/The Image Bank/ Getty Images.

177: Leonard de Selva/CORBIS.

177: Paul A. Souders/CORBIS.

183: Diana Sullada.

186: Kevin Fleming/CORBIS.

187: Karen Kasmauski/CORBIS.

188: By kind permission of the Old Ebbitt Grill.

189: Philip Gould/CORBIS.

191: David Katzenstein/CORBIS.

196: David Honor. By kind permission of Shaw's Crab House.

195: By kind permission, Fore Street.

200: Bill Murtagh, by kind permission, Rodney's Oyster House.

207: By kind permission, Wright Brothers, Borough Market, London.

206: C. Murtin/photocuisine/ CORBIS.

212: Harald Jahn/CORBIS.

215: Nicoloso/photocuisine/CORBIS.

226: By kind permission, Michelle Quance/ michellequance.com

244: By kind permission, Maria B. Petersen.

245: Keith Lanpher Photography/ lanpher.com

255: Brilynn Ferguson/ brilynnferguson.com

The eldest Oyster looked at him,
But never a word he said:
The eldest Oyster winked his eye,
And shook his heavy head —
Meaning to say he did not choose
To leave the oyster-bed.

– LEWIS CARROLL, *The Walrus & The Carpenter*

INDEX

ABOUT THE AUTHOR

PATRICK McMURRAY is the proprietor of The Ceílí Cottage, a beloved and much lauded restaurant in Toronto's Leslieville neighborhood. He is holder of the *Guinness World Records* title as the world's fastest shucker, and multiple national, regional and international championships. His now legendary Starfish Oyster Bed and Grill was visited by diners and passionate oyster lovers from around the world, many of whom have followed adventures in oystering from coast to coast in North America, and around the world. You can follow Shucker Paddy at @ShuckerPaddy. And, if you are lucky, you may now and again find him at 43° 39' 48" N, 79°19'40" W — 269 feet above sea level.

Photography by Brilynn Ferguson

KIM HARKNESS
Developmental and Project Editor

YVONNE KOO
Designer

ZANE KANEPS
Creative, Editorial, and Design Consultant

RACHEL PENNINGTON-LITTLE
Picture Research

The publisher wishes to thank Tracy Bordian for her considered editorial advice, and Addy Alimajstorovic for location photography. And to Patrick McMurray — a passionate and creative advocate for the oyster, and a damn good photographer, too.

The publisher also wishes to thank the following individuals, who contributed significantly to the previous edition of this title, first published in 2007: Cynthia David, Inderjit Deogun, Sandra Hall, Alison Maclean, Beth Martin, Wanda Nowakowska, and Diana Sullada.